Only Entertainment

Everyone knows what entertainment is, yet we still find it hard to define. In *Only Entertainment*, Richard Dyer argues that we have to start any analysis of entertainment by understanding it *as entertainment*, as part of a 'common sense' which is always historically and culturally constructed. In a series of lucid and provocative essays, Dyer investigates, without rejecting aesthetics or ideological criticism, the social construction of entertainment.

All of the essays relate to – and perhaps helped lay the foundations for – current debates in gender studies, lesbian and gay studies, and the turn towards cultural studies. Dyer's subjects range from classical ballet to disco, from star pin-ups to pornography, from TV classic serials to camp. His introduction places the writings in the context of current cultural debates, and the concluding essay links ideas of pleasure to the politics of sexuality.

Richard Dyer is Senior Lecturer in Film Studies at the University of Warwick. He has written numerous articles on film, television, cultural and gender studies, and is the author of *Light Entertainment* (1973), *Stars* (1979), *Heavenly Bodies* (1987), and *Now You See It* (Routledge 1990). He is the co-editor with Ginette Vincendeau of *Popular European Cinema* (Routledge 1992).

Only Entertainment

Richard Dyer

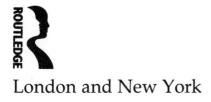

London and New York

First published 1992
by Routledge
11 New Fetter Lane, London EC4P 4EE

Simultaneously published in the USA and Canada
by Routledge
a division of Routledge, Chapman and Hall, Inc.
29 West 35th Street, New York, NY 10001

Typeset in 10 on 12 point Palatino by
Florencetype, Kewstoke, Avon
Printed in Great Britain by
Butler & Tanner Ltd, Frome & London

British Library Cataloguing in Publication Data
Dyer, Richard
  Only entertainment.
  I. Title
  306.4

Library of Congress Cataloging in Publication Data
Dyer, Richard.
  Only entertainment/ Richard Dyer.
    p.   cm.
  Includes bibliographical references.
  1. Performing arts—Social aspects. 2. Popular culture. I. Title.
PN1590. S6D94   1992
306.4'84—dc20   91–47107

ISBN 0–415–05716–7   0–415–05717–5 (pbk)

To Rosalind
for all the rainbows

Contents

Preface   ix

1 Introduction   1

2 The notion of entertainment   11

3 Entertainment and utopia   17

4 Quality pleasures   35

5 Classical ballet: a bit of uplift   41

6 *The Sound of Music*   45

7 *Sweet Charity*   61

8 Four films of Lana Turner   65

9 *The Son of the Sheik*   99

10 Don't look now: the instabilities of the male pin-up   103

11 Coming to terms: gay pornography   121

12 It's being so camp as keeps us going   135

13 In defence of disco   149

14 Getting over the rainbow: identity and pleasure in gay
    cultural politics   159

Index   173

Preface

The essays in this book are attempts to understand the qualities of things that we label entertainment. Although written over a period of approximately twenty years, ranging from analyses of particular films through studies of entertainment genres to ideas about ways of life, and published in a variety of journalistic and academic contexts, they do share a common project informed by certain basic positions, which may be summarized as follows:

I am glad that things that are entertainment are available in societies and happy that we avail ourselves of them. In other words, I have no problem with there being a category of cultural production known as entertainment. In the earlier essays, I often felt a need to defend the category from puritanical and political attack; sometimes more recently I have felt that in some intellectual circles, it is morality and politics that need defence against born-again hedonists.

Because it is so easy to use the term, I don't think we easily know what it means and involves. At the same time, I am resistant to understanding it in terms which attempt to explain it with reference to that which is not entertainment, to privilege the intellectual paradigms and 'depth models' of, notably, economics, ideology and the unconscious, over the evidence of experience and consciousness.

Because it is a simple term, I do not regard either the texts of entertainment or people's responses to them as simple, uniform, or uncontradictory. I have on the contrary often wanted to explore their complexity and contradictoriness as an intrinsic part of understanding the phenomenon of entertainment.

Because something is entertainment, I do not assume it is therefore fine. There are vicious pleasures as well as benign ones; there are prices paid for giving us pleasure (e.g. racist jokes; demeaning pin-ups)

x *Only Entertainment*

that are not redeemed by the pleasure they give. Nor is there virtue simply in being complex and contradictory. Defence and understanding of entertainment in general do not mean being uncritical of it in particular.

I feel somewhat embarrassed in the current postmodern mood to admit that these positions have been modified, nuanced and changed in accord with changes in the political–intellectual climate but they have not been in a constant state of flux and mix 'n' match uncertainty. They are, of course, like all ideas, inevitably partial, that is, incomplete and from a position, but there is nothing new in saying that.

*   *   *

Apart from corrections of minor factual errors, I have not altered these essays from how they originally appeared. At the end of most essays, I have appended a brief and highly selective list of articles that deal with similar or related issues, sometimes explicitly taking issue with or building on my remarks.

The acknowledgements due to academic friends and colleagues are too numerous to re-establish thoroughly with a collection like this. The people I should like to thank here are those who commissioned or encouraged many of these writings, notably Roger Baker, Rosalind Brunt, Jane Clarke, Jim Hillier, Sally Townsend and Christopher Williams.

*   *   *

I would like to acknowledge the following for stills or other illustrations: BBC Photo Library (figure 4.1); BFI Stills, Posters and Design (figures 3.1, 3.2, 3.3, 3.4, 6.1, 6.2, 7.1, 7.2, 8.2, 8.3, 8.7, 8.8, 8.10, 9.1, 10,2, 10.4, 12.2, 12.3, 12.4, 14.1); Granada Television (figure 4.2); MGM Ltd (figure 10.1); and Playgirl Inc. (figures 10.5, 10.10).

1 Introduction

Everyone knows what entertainment is. It is obvious.

Except that as soon as we begin to talk about it we get into a muddle. Let me leave aside the application of the term to the many things that entertain people: having friends to dinner and to stay, studying maths or deconstructive theory, pursuing sports, hobbies and so on. For the purposes of this volume, 'entertainment' is confined to its application to cultural products, 'the arts' and 'the media'. Moreover, to describe our response to the latter we often use 'entertaining' broadly interchangeably with 'enjoyable' or such phrases as 'I like it'. In that sense any cultural product any person likes is for them 'entertaining', and 'entertainment' is a category of response not of things – we cannot lay down a rule that only some cultural products entertain since they (virtually) all entertain someone. However, what remains unclear is what we mean by using the term 'entertainment', why we want to call some responses to cultural products those of being 'entertained' (and hence why in practice we do transfer the quality of being 'entertainment' to those products themselves).

Of course *we* know what we mean, but we find it hard to say what we mean.

Entertainment is difficult to define *because* everyone knows what it is, because it is a common-sense idea. Common sense is the cornerstone of day-to-day thought and talk, and for that very reason it is resistant to the probings of those who want to ask what such-and-such means. Questioning common sense, however sympathetically, stops the flow, unsettles the comfortable taken-for-grantedness of the ways in which we habitually make sense of our lives and thoughts and feelings, to ourselves and with others. Hence the halting quality of discussion about entertainment, a haltingness easily escalating into irritation:

'I must get back in time for *The Generation Game*.'
'I know, it's great isn't it? Why do you like it?'
'What do you mean?'
'Well, what do you like about it?'

'Well, it's entertaining, isn't it?'

'Yes, but why is it entertaining? What's entertaining about it?'

'Well, I don't know, it's fun, it's a laugh, it's enjoyable, it's . . . well, it's just entertaining.'

'I know, but what is it about it that's entertaining?'

'Oh I don't know, it just *is*.'

'But there must be some reason . . .'

'Oh Richard, why do you have to go on about things? Can't you just accept that it is entertaining and leave it at that?'

The notion of entertainment is especially liable to provoke such exchanges, because part of its meaning is anti-seriousness, against coming on heavy about things. It still perhaps carries a guilty conscience. It rejects the claims of morality, politics and aesthetics in a culture which still accords these high status. It is born of a society that both considers leisure and pleasure to be secondary and even inferior to the businesses of producing and reproducing, work and family, and yet invests much energy, desire and money into promoting them. Equally, as Anita Skwara (1992) has pointed out, counter-capitalist views, as embodied in Marxism, themselves secondarize leisure and pleasure to labour and production and hence have been able to provide little support for the justified exploration of these areas. No wonder that entertainment has to be an end point in discourse, a block, its own justification, nothing more to be said, obvious.

To examine what entertainment is may not itself be what is usually thought of as entertainment. This is partly because most attempts to take entertainment seriously do so in ways that avoid treating it *as* entertainment. Morag Shiach notes in the related (but not conterminous) discursive field of 'popular culture' how

> analyses . . . are always connected to, and motivated by, problems and perceived limitations within the dominant culture, rather than emerging from an engagement with the material forms of popular culture themselves.
>
> (1989: 6)

As a result much of what is written seems not to be *about* its ostensible subject and this is if anything still more true of 'entertainment', where the issue of what it is seems so often to be side-stepped. There is a very long tradition, traced by, among many others, Leo Lowenthal (1961) and Patrick Brantlinger (1983), which for the most part condemns entertainment for being entertainment, distraction, pleasure, triviality. Some of this does at least have the merit, for all its hostility, of trying to describe what entertainment is. Among more recent examples, for instance, the equivocal discussion in Weimar Germany of '*Zerstreuung*', glossed by Heide Schlüpmann (summarizing Kracauer 1926) as 'abandoning oneself to pure appearances, to the "dazzle", renouncing concern with meaning or "content" ' (1982: 46), was attempting to describe the delight of the new mass medium of cinema. I want to look in this introduction, however, at the ways an apparent concern with entertainment in debates since the 1960s has all the same often not addressed entertainment *qua* entertainment.

One way has been to take the stance of saying that such-and-such is entertaining, granted and that's fine, but it is also something else, and then talking about the something else. Film studies have been particularly rich in this 'but also' approach. Time and again we are not told why Westerns are exciting, why horror films horrify, why weepies make us cry, but instead are told that, while they are exciting, horrifying, or tearjerking, the films also deal with history, society, psychology, gender roles, indeed, the meaning of life. The growth of studies of Hollywood movies in terms of their directors has often been oddly placed in relation to the films' entertainingness. It's not that such studies do not tell us something about the films, often a great deal, but they seldom say why the films are entertaining. The model of showing how the text makes profound statements despite also being entertaining (no longer spat at as an incidental aim) remains strong.

What lurks here is the distinction between art and entertainment. Many would argue that entertainment and art are not distinguishable, and indeed as discrete categories of product this is in many ways true. What one person terms art another terms entertainment and vice versa, and we'll probably never agree on which is which. 'Entertainment', especially preceded by 'just', is often used as a term to deny or discount something's aesthetic and ideological qualities, just as the art label often prevents people from seeing how enjoyable something is. As a description of products, as a way of categorizing them, above all as a way of discriminating between them in terms of value, art:entertainment is a dubious and often deadly distinction. Yet it remains a powerful discursive presence. The film-studies project of insisting that Hollywood movies are not just entertainment in fact reaffirms the art:entertainment distinction even while disputing its application. We know what we mean when we say (or when someone else says) that *x* is both art and entertainment, that it is the one as well as being the other, or that *y* deserves to be categorized as art rather than as entertainment. The terms have meanings and implications that we continue to employ even when we are disputing their application in given cases. Moreover, culture is produced in the context of that distinction. The obligations on Hollywood to be entertaining and on state-funded films to be artistic are real ones, however much they may be resisted or transcended in practice. It is the implications of the obligation to be entertaining, as carried in the texts themselves and the expectations of the audience, that have been the focus of the essays collected here.[1]

A second common form of intellectual avoidance of entertainment *qua* entertainment, psychoanalysis, is recognizable by its preference for the words 'pleasure' and 'desire' over 'entertainment'. This is due perhaps to an instinctive recognition that 'entertainment' is a notion referring to public discourses of enjoyment, whereas psychoanalysis tends to favour enjoyment experienced as private (with the private generally presumed to be more real than the public). The psychoanalytic approach to plea-sure has many variations, but all locate pleasure in the unconscious (thus by definition beyond the reach of common sense) and in versions of the human child's entry into the social organization of bodily func-tions and relations (and especially the prohibitions, misconceptions and traumas surrounding this). Often the reference to the latter in psychoa-nalytically inclined accounts functions much as 'deep meaning' does in more traditional forms of criticism, telling us what a text's or medium's pleasures really are despite what they appear to be.

Given its dominance in the field of cultural, and especially film, studies and its absence by and large from the essays collected here, I had better say something further about psychoanalysis. It is clear that no white person living in Europe, North America, or Australasia in the twentieth century is likely to be untouched by psychoanalytic notions – they were designed to explain us to ourselves and have been successful. Popular and high culture alike are drenched in them and I find it hard to imagine *not* thinking, and experiencing, child–parent relations as cen-tral, persistent and libidinal in human subjectivity and *not* recognizing that much of that subjectivity is neither present nor even readily avail-able to consciousness. Thus I have no quarrel with work such as Mary Ann Doane's study of the 1940s woman's film, where she defines her aim as 'to trace a coincidence of cinematic scenarios and psychoanalytic scenarios of female subjectivity' (1987: 21), since the former were clearly produced within, and promoted the development of, the culture of the latter. Like her, however, only more so, I would want to eschew using psychoanalysis 'as a pure or neutral metalanguage or methodology' (ibid.).

There are considerable problems with treating psychoanalysis as a master discourse of truth, especially in the Lacanian variant so influen-tial on film studies and that bit of media studies that abuts it.[2] The appeal of psychoanalysis on its introduction to the field lay in its promise to explain why socialists and feminists liked things they thought they ought not to, and in the fact that it was the only such theory around. But promises and the rhetoric of theory are not them-selves reasons to believe in something; one has to have warrant for such belief, otherwise it is only 'belief'. Psychoanalysis is not amenable to empirical investigation nor is it internally coherent, two characteristics it has alternately tried to disprove or paraded as virtues. Psychoanalysis is normatively phallocentric and homophobic, though some valiantly aver (without demonstrating) that it can be used as a theory of these qualities. Apart from such intrinsic difficulties, there is a problem with applying what is a theory, and a therapy, focused on the specificity of individual development, to a generalized gendered subjectivity and *a fortiori* to collectivities, institutions and apparatuses, such as entertainment and popular culture. Given all that, what remains is faith.

The parallel between psychoanalysis and religion is a well-known one. Both take as their object something that by definition cannot be proved or disproved to exist: the unconscious or God. Both elaborate arcane systems of discourse, theological and ritualistic, in which obscurity and incantation (the endless repetition of key terms and tropes) play crucial roles. Religion, however, has at least this merit: most people in the world believe in some form of it. Academic psychoanalysis on the other hand is highly marginal even within the west, let alone the world, and Lacanianism is the outer margin of the margin. (This may constitute its glamour for some, but there is a difference between a chosen marginality and an enforced one based on gender, ethnicity, or sexuality.) Why it came to such prominence in 1970s/1980s cultural analysis is a history yet to be written; why it, a depth model *par excellence*, survives into the moment of postmodernism is also an interesting question to be addressed.

Psychoanalysis by and large took a negative view of pleasure. 'It is said that analysing pleasure, or beauty, destroys it. That is the intention of this article', observed Laura Mulvey (1985: 306) in one of the most influential, and best, articles of the tendency. This negative view has informed a great deal of the broadly left discussion of entertainment, even when it is not psychoanalytically inclined. Some of this discussion takes the time-honoured view of entertainment as the sugar on the pill of the real meaning and purpose of the cultural product in question, which in this case is 'ideology'. Whether canvassing the need for the left to use entertainment forms as the vector to reach the mass of the people, condemning the dominant ideology for its unabashed recourse to entertainment for the promulgation of existing class, gender and race relations, or joining the two in (rightly) characterizing entertainment as a site of ideological struggle, such accounts in general take what the sugar is as unproblematic.

Two directions, however, have sought to address the issue of entertainment as entertainment. One seeks to define entertainment as itself an ideology. James Linton, for instance, starts and finishes with a sugaring-the-pill position, noting the way the idea of entertainment, shared by producers and audiences alike, may 'lower [the latter's] "psychic guard" ' (1978: 17) and concluding with the stark option for film-makers either to 'realize the "socially conscious entertainment film", or pronounce it a basic contradiction in terms' (ibid.: 18). In between, however, he does offer an account of entertainment focused on absorption in narrative, identification with stars and characters, and the pleasure of reassurance. The latter is assumed to be inherently conservative, partly because comfort and stability themselves have low status in left discourses that valorize struggle and revolution, partly because such discourses assume that anything produced by capitalist industry must necessarily reassure audiences about the rightness of capitalism (a point disputed in Lovell 1980). Nevertheless this account does at least take seriously the qualities of absorption, identification and reassurance that are major aspects of entertainment.

The second direction shares the concern of writers like Linton with the ideology of entertainment, but is also anxious not to throw the baby of enjoyment out with the bathwater of ideological entertainment. What is at issue is conceptualizing radical pleasure. Some canvass the pleasures of resistance and struggle themselves, 'serious pleasures' as R. L. Rutsky and Justin Wyatt (1990) dub them, while others (myself in the article on pornography included here) long for pleasure unclouded by misgiving. More interesting, and influential, have been definitions of a kind of enjoyment that evades the constrictions of 'conservative' pleasure. I would include here, fully acknowledging their enormous differences, the renewal of interest in the '*Zerstreuung*' mentioned above (pp. 2–3) and in Mikhail Bakhtin's notion of the 'carnivalesque' (1968) as well as Roland Barthes's distinction between the '*plaisir*' of order and the '*jouissance*' of abandon (1975). What these share is an interest in, and valorization of, kinds of pleasure which seem to break free from the discipline of formally well-behaved narrativity and staid, coherent points of view.

In alerting us to different constructions of enjoyment, these accounts of what I'll term 'unruly delight' are enormously useful, even if in practice they tend to validate certain kinds of avant-gardism or 'authentic' popular culture at the expense of 'entertainment', rather than tracing its presence in the latter alongside more evidently orderly enjoyment. What worries me more about notions of unruly delight is their recourse to a fantasy much beloved of very responsible, cerebral people, the fantasy of being beyond responsibility and cerebration, the fantasy of regression. This is not to deny the appeal of that fantasy, the reality of the delight of abandon, but to query the implication that abandon is not itself a social construction. At the least, abandon derives its force from coexistence with orderliness, carnivalesque overturning depends upon there being things to turn over, and so on. Moreover, on inspection the forms that unruly delight takes turn out to be every bit as historically and culturally specific as those of orderly enjoyment: on the one hand, deploying the figure of the artist as wild child, there is a familiar package of romantic/modernist devices, and on the other, in the absence of the peasants in Bakhtin's theory, we find a celebration of today's peasantry – black people, or 'the feminine', or queers (though not the black bourgeoisie, or actual ordinary women, or people calling themselves lesbian or gay) as the embodiment of this inchoate pleasure.

In other words, whatever the theorization, there is a recourse to a notion of an unsocialized pleasure. In less theorized work this takes the form of a simple assertion that something is, after all, enjoyable and why not, even if it is also ideologically unsound, a kind of born-again hedonism, champing against the joylessness of political correctness. This is to assume, once again, that entertainment is already unproblematically known, neutral and given, is 'only' entertainment.

Yet entertainment offers certain pleasures not others, proposes that we find such-and-such delightful, teaches us enjoyment – including the enjoyment of unruly delight. It works with the desires that circulate in a given society at a given time, neither wholly constructing those desires nor merely reflecting desires produced elsewhere; it plays a major role in the social construction of happiness. We have to understand it itself, neither take it as given nor assume that behind it lies something more important.

Rather than look, as most of what I have been discussing does, to other discourses to explain (explain away?) entertainment, we might be well advised to listen, really listen, to the discourse of entertainment itself. In chapter 2, 'The notion of entertainment' (itself based on a longer, unpublished manuscript), I take the ideas of Molière in his play *The Critique of 'The School for Wives'* as a crystallization of many of the assumptions about what theatre should be, assumptions couched in common-sense language that define the very basis of theatre as entertainment in terms that were then new and controversial but are now utterly everyday; in chapter 3, 'Entertainment and utopia', I take one of the most commonly said things about 'entertainment', that it is 'escapist', as a concept for analysing it. More generally I have sought throughout to listen to my own responses and those of my friends and colleagues[3] as well as to the texts of entertainment themselves to see what notions of entertainment circulate and how they provide understandings of the enterprise of entertainment.

I have of course brought something to bear on all the above. One has to make common sense strange in order to be able to see it. The very act of naming and describing makes it strange, refuses to take it for granted. Insisting on its relativity, its historical and cultural specificity, does the same. Equally it is evident from my choice of vocabulary, form of argument and so on – even when I have not made it explicit – that I have brought certain personal, political and intellectual paradigms to bear, such as the notion that people have a material place in society which limits but also makes possible certain cultural options for them, or the assumption of the operation of unequal though not uniquely one-way power in social relations, or the interest in the contradictions of cultural products, their lack of ideological uniformity both as texts and in how they are read and enjoyed. I do not operate very happily on the terrain of big generalization; reality exists in the specific and concrete, but though I do not go on about it, I am far from believing that the specific and concrete, the obvious, nay 'entertainment', speak for themselves. Each of us makes them speak from what we bring to bear on them, which is theory (if not Theory). I wanted in these essays to use both theory and listening to make sense of the entertainment of entertainment.

NOTES

1 'Entertainment' is also part of the professional ideology, the day-to-day assumptions and habits of thought, of cultural producers. Work needs to be done on this area (beyond noting that the word 'entertainment' is used a lot) and on the degree of fit or mismatch between producers', texts' and audiences' definitions of entertainment.
2 For a brief account of Lacanian psychoanalysis in a film studies context, see Kuhn 1982: 45–9.
3 I do not take my world to be the world, but nor do I feel, as John Caughie observes of much writing on the subject, 'that popular culture is what *other* people like' (1986: 170). (There is plenty of entertainment that means nothing to me – rock 'n' roll, opera, football, all but British soaps – but everyone discriminates within entertainment and popular culture and anyway I don't write about them.)

REFERENCES

Bakhtin, Mikhail (1968) *Rabelais and His World*, Cambridge, MA: MIT Press.
Barthes, Roland (1975) *The Pleasure of the Text*, New York: Hill & Wang.
Brantlinger, Patrick (1983) *Bread and Circuses: Theories of Mass Culture as Social Decay*, Ithaca, NY: Cornell University Press.
Caughie, John (1986) 'Popular culture: notes and revisions', in Colin MacCabe (ed.) *High Theory/Low Culture*, Manchester: Manchester University Press, 156–71.
Doane, Mary Ann (1987) *The Desire to Desire: The Woman's Film of the 1940s*, London: Macmillan.
Kracauer, Siegfried (1926) 'Kult der Zerstreuung', *Frankfurter Zeitung*, 4 March; translated in *New German Critique* 40.
Kuhn, Annette (1982) *Women's Pictures*, London: Routledge & Kegan Paul.
Linton, James (1978) 'But it's only a movie', *Jump Cut* 17: 16–19.
Lovell, Terry (1980) *Pictures of Reality*, London: British Film Institute.
Lowenthal, Leo (1961) *Literature, Popular Culture and Society*, Englewood Cliffs, NJ: Prentice-Hall.
Mulvey, Laura (1985) 'Visual pleasure and narrative cinema', in Bill

Nichols (ed.) *Movies and Methods*, Berkeley, CA: University of California Press, 305–15.

Rutsky, R. L. and Wyatt, Justin (1990) 'Serious pleasures: cinematic pleasure and the notion of fun', *Cinema Journal* 30 (1): 3–19.

Schlüpmann, Heide (1982) 'Kinosucht', *Frauen und Film* 33: 45–52.

Shiach, Morag (1989) *Discourse on Popular Culture: Class, Gender and History in Cultural Analysis, 1730 to the Present*, Oxford: Polity Press.

Skwara, Anita (1992) 'Film stars do not shine in the sky over Poland: the absence of popular cinema in Poland', in Richard Dyer and Ginette Vincendeau (eds) *Popular European Cinema*, London: Routledge, pp. 219–30.

FURTHER READING

Collins, Jim (1989) *Uncommon Cultures: Popular Culture and Post-modernism*, London: Routledge.

Modleski, Tania (ed.) (1986) *Studies in Entertainment*, Bloomington, Ind.: Indiana University Press.

Ross, Andrew (1989) *No Respect: Intellectuals and Popular Culture*, New York and London: Routledge.

2 The notion of entertainment

Uranie: [Molière] doesn't care if people attack his plays, as long as plenty of people go to them.

*   *   *

Dorante: It's a skill, making people laugh.

*   *   *

Uranie: When I go to a show, I just consider the things that move me, and if I've enjoyed myself, I don't start worrying about whether I ought to have or whether Aristotle's rules forbid me to laugh.

*   *   *

Dorante: Surely the rule of all rules is to please?
                          Molière: *The Critique of 'The School for Wives'*

The clown with his pants falling down,
Or the lights on the lady in tights,
Or the scene where the villain is mean,
   That's entertainment!
It might be a scene like you see on the screen,
A swain getting slain for the love of a queen,
Some great Shakespearean scene
Where a ghost and a prince meet
And everything ends in mincemeat.
            Howard Dietz and Arthur Schwartz: 'That's Entertainment!'

Entertainment, show business, Variety are not terms that are normally much thought about. Indeed they are often the final point in a conversation: 'Well anyway I like it. It's good entertainment' – said defensively when you are praising an unfashionable film in intellectual circles; or else the tag, now a comic cliché, used in backstage musicals at crucial points in the plot: 'That's show business!' Nothing more needs to be said: we all share a common-sense notion of what entertainment is. Yet precisely because it is such a final or absolute notion, it is very hard to define.

You can't get at it simply by listing examples. The song 'That's Entertainment!' by Dietz and Schwartz is a veritable compendium of what may be considered entertainment and lists, without any apparent sense of contradiction, *Hamlet* and *Oedipus Rex* alongside 'the clown with his pants falling down' and 'the lights on the lady in tights'. If all these things can be entertainment, then clearly entertainment is not so much a category of things as an attitude towards things.

We can best come to an understanding of what this attitude is by a series of negations.

First, entertainment is not simply a way of describing something found equally in all societies at all times. Song and dance in tribal societies, for instance, are specifically tied to religious and utilitarian purposes, placating the gods or conjuring up rain. The pageants and amusements of medieval Europe were part of the whole pattern of social life and built right into the organization of the calendar, governed by the Church and tied to seasonal – hence, economic – festivals. Where in tribal society song and dance sought to have an effect on life, in medieval society they celebrated it in a systematically structured way. Our entertainment may, of course, do both these things, but it is not in any coherent way associated with serious metaphysical or ceremonial practice. On the other hand, it is different from the growth of amusements and diversions in courtly society. Unlike them, modern entertainment is not simply a way of staving off days of boredom for a leisured class nor is it simply an adjunct to social intercourse.

A key figure in the emergence of 'entertainment' is Molière, who in having to elaborate a defence of his plays developed a new definition of what the theatre should do. The Church had attacked him for not edifying, the salons for his refusal to conform to the taste for polite *divertissement* and the critics for not obeying the rules of art. His defence was to deny that those concepts of what he should do were relevant to his real purpose, which was to provide pleasure – and the definition of *that* was to be decided by 'the people'. Against salons, Church and critics Molière set the court (which at this time was characterized by an impotent aristocracy and a newly recruited bourgeoisie who actually ran the country) and the gallery; against received élite opinion he asserted populism. In so doing, he severed art from entertainment – not, it is true, in his own practice but in theory. Entertainment became identified with what was not art, not serious, not refined. This distinction remains with us – art is what is edifying, élitist, refined, difficult, whilst entertainment is hedonistic, democratic, vulgar, easy. That the distinction is harmful, false to the best in both what is called art and what is called entertainment, has often been commented upon. But it remains one built into our education and, as we shall see, the decisions of television programmers.

Entertainment is also a part of 'leisure'. This is a specifically modern idea and is again best defined negatively, as is done, for instance, by Kenneth Roberts:

> Leisure time can be defined as time that is not obligated, and leisure activities can be defined as activities that are non-obligatory. At work, a man's time is not his own and his behaviour is not responsive purely to his own whims. Outside work, there are certain duties that men are obliged, either by custom or law, to fulfil, such as the obligations that an individual has towards his family. When these obligations have been met, a man has 'free time' in which his behaviour is dictated by his own will and preference, and it is here that leisure is found.
>
> (Roberts 1970: 6)

Leisure and entertainment are separate from and in opposition to work and domestic cares. In a functional analysis, leisure can be seen either as a way of compensating for the dreariness of work or else as the passivity attendant on industrial labour (cf Wilensky 1962). But the richness and variety of the actual forms of leisure suggest that leisure should also be seen as the creation of meaning in a world in which work and the daily round are characterized by drudgery, insistence and meaninglessness.

Entertainment is a specific aspect of this leisure. It is provided and it is paid for, and in this it is unlike talking, hobbies, sex and games. It derives in its characteristic form – the string of short items, with or without link-man, the popular and vulgar reference, the implicit sexuality and open sentimentality – from the development of entertainment in the pubs and clubs patronized by the urban working class.[1] This form has, of course, been fed by the continuing traditions of bourgeois amusement – operetta, musical comedy, parlour songs – but this has only tended to refine or embellish (and sometimes emasculate) the form, not to dominate it. Telescoping history in this way does, of course, miss out all sorts of nuance, but it does help us to grasp the specificity of the generalized contemporary notion, 'entertainment'.

If we now glance at a couple of official statements from BBC and ITV respectively we shall observe that this notion informs the thinking of these companies – not so much what they actually think or say, but what is implied in the sort of things they find it necessary to say publicly.

First, Tom Sloan's attempt to define light entertainment at a BBC lunchtime lecture:[2]

> We have Drama and Features and Arts Features and General Features and Documentaries *and* Talk and Current Affairs, to name but a few. But I believe that a great mass of people want to treat their television sets as a means of escape, and never more so than at the present time.

I remember one wet Sunday, in 1961, driving to Liverpool to see a new group called the Beatles give a concert for their fan club which we televised. For the first time in my life, I saw the industrial north of England, the rows of terraced houses, fronting on to the cobbled roads, glistening in the rain. The sheer ghastliness of it all was overpowering, but on the roof of every house, there was a television aerial. Antennae reaching for escape to another world. And, heaven knows, why not?

So my job is to organize a stream of output which is primarily intended to please and relax those who wish to receive it. In other words, to entertain.

As usual, we end up with that explain-all, 'to entertain', but before that we may note the careful distinction of entertainment from art and information, and the distinction in terms of escape from the horrors of life. We should note, too, the rather patronizing tone of the man who provides entertainment for 'a great mass of people'. If we see entertainment from the point of view of the providers, then we are asking questions like, How do you distract people from the horrors of everyday life? What is strong enough to shut it out for a while? How do you bring a little sparkle into the drabness? and also, How can you get on their side, not alienate them with art or education? This is the peculiar inflection of the responsible voice in mass entertainment and must have an influence on any aesthetic approach we make to it.

An ITV pronouncement[3] is equally revealing:

> It is common to write as though comedy and light entertainment were much the same thing. It is true that they have a common objective – to provide relaxing[4] entertainment. It is true, too, that in a country in which there are remnants of a puritan tradition the two are still sometimes lumped together as though they belonged in some rather disreputable bargain-basement of broadcasting. Nothing could be further from the truth. No aspect of broadcasting calls for greater skills or harder work from producers, directors and performers than the business of earning laughs or mounting an exciting production number.

Here there is an explicitly apologetic note, as is frequent enough in pronouncements from ITV, vulnerable to the attack of commercial exploitation. Their first answer, interestingly enough, is to defend the criticism of puritanism by a puritanical insistence on work, professionalism. This notion, however, is superseded in the next paragraph by an even more powerful argument:

> There is still a shortage of light entertainment programmes of the highest quality. But it would be wrong to exaggerate. Many programmes have given a great deal of pleasure to very many people.

Populism has crept back, for the logic behind this is that as long as people enjoy it (or rather, as long as 'very many people' turn it on) it doesn't matter much what it's like.

Both these statements rely on a notion of entertainment such as has been sketched, but also reveal the peculiar quality of mass entertainment, provided by a specialist profession for people conceived of as an undifferentiated mass. Hence the philistinism and self-indulgence implicit in the notion are not tempered by the real vulgarity and consciousness of oppression of the people, but by the power of professional standards and the sensitivity of power to public opinion (both of which tend to temper vulgarity and indulgence in the name of responsibility) and more still by what producers think constitutes the entertainment needs of the working class.

Television light entertainment is founded on a very specific idea of what entertainment is in a modern industrial society. We must now look at the aesthetic consequences of this.

NOTES

This chapter was originally published in 1973 in *Light Entertainment*, BFI Television Monograph 2, London: British Film Institute; this monograph *does* go on to look at the aesthetic consequences referred to above.

1 A particularly interesting connection between the industrial experience and the actual form of entertainment is made in McLean 1965.
2 11 December 1969. Published as a pamphlet by the BBC.
3 *Independent Television Authority, Annual Report and Accounts, 1969–70*, London: HMSO, 15.
4 Note that both extracts use this word almost involuntarily. Its implication of prior tension links entertainment directly with the stresses of work and life.

REFERENCES

McLean, Albert F. Jr (1965) *American Vaudeville as Ritual*, Lexington: University Press of Kentucky.
Roberts, Kenneth (1970) *Leisure*, London: Longman.
Wilensky, H. L. (1962) 'Labour and Leisure: intellectual traditions', *Industrial Relations* 1 (2).

3 Entertainment and utopia

This article is about musicals as entertainment. I don't necessarily want to disagree with those who would claim that musicals are also 'something else' (e.g. 'Art') or argue that entertainment itself is only a product of 'something more important' (e.g. political/economic manipulation, psychological forces), but I want to put the emphasis here on entertainment as entertainment. Musicals were predominantly conceived of, by producers and audiences alike, as 'pure entertainment' – the *idea* of entertainment was a prime determinant on them. Yet because entertainment is a common-sense, 'obvious' idea, what is really meant and implied by it never gets discussed.

Musicals are one of a whole string of forms – music hall, variety, TV spectaculars, pantomime, cabaret, etc. – that are usually summed up by the term 'show biz'. The idea of entertainment I want to examine here is most centrally embodied by these forms, although I believe that it can also be seen at work, *mutatis mutandis*, in other forms and I suggest below, informally, how this might be so. However, it is probably true to say that 'show biz' is the most thoroughly entertainment-oriented of all types of performance, and that notions of myth, art, instruction, dream and ritual may be equally important, even at the conscious level, with regard to, say, Westerns, the news, soap opera, or rock music.

It is important, I think, to stress the cultural and historical specificity of entertainment. The kinds of performance produced by professional entertainment are different in audience, performers and above all intention to the kinds of performance produced in tribal, feudal, or socialist societies. It is not possible here to provide the detailed historical and anthropological argument to back this up, but I hope the differences will suggest themselves when I say that entertainment is a type of performance produced for profit, performed before a generalized audience (the 'public'), by a trained, paid group who do nothing else but produce performances which have the sole (conscious) aim of providing pleasure.

Because entertainment is produced by professional entertainers, it is also largely defined by them. That is to say, although entertainment is part of the coinage of everyday thought, none the less how it is defined, what it is assumed to be, is basically decided by those people responsible (paid) for providing it in concrete form. Professional entertainment is the dominant agency for defining what entertainment is. This does not mean, however, that it *simply* reproduces and expresses patriarchal capitalism. There is the usual struggle between capital (the backers) and labour (the performers) over control of the product, and professional entertainment is unusual in that: (1) it is in the business of producing forms not things, and (2) the workforce (the performers themselves) is in a better position to determine the form of its product than are, say, secretaries or car workers. The fact that professional entertainment has been by and large conservative in this century should not blind us to the implicit struggle within it, and looking beyond class to divisions of sex and race, we should note the important role of structurally subordinate groups in society – women, blacks, gays – in the development and definition of entertainment. In other words, show business's relationship to the demands of patriarchal capitalism is a complex one. Just as it does not simply 'give the people what they want' (since it actually defines those wants), so, as a relatively autonomous mode of cultural production, it does not simply reproduce unproblematically patriarchal-capitalist ideology. Indeed, it is precisely on seeming to achieve both these often opposed functions simultaneously that its survival largely depends.

Two of the taken-for-granted descriptions of entertainment, as 'escape' and as 'wish-fulfilment', point to its central thrust, namely, utopianism. Entertainment offers the image of 'something better' to escape into, or something we want deeply that our day-to-day lives don't provide. Alternatives, hopes, wishes – these are the stuff of utopia, the sense that things could be better, that something other than what is can be imagined and maybe realized.

Entertainment does not, however, present models of utopian worlds, as in the classic utopias of Thomas More, William Morris, *et al.* Rather the utopianism is contained in the feelings it embodies. It presents, head-on as it were, what utopia would feel like rather than how it would be organized. It thus works at the level of sensibility, by which I mean an affective code that is characteristic of, and largely specific to, a given mode of cultural production.

This code uses both representational and, importantly, non-representational signs. There is a tendency to concentrate on the former, and clearly it would be wrong to overlook them – stars are nicer than we are, characters more straightforward than people we know, situations more soluble than those we encounter. All this we recognize through representational signs. But we also recognize qualities in non-representational signs – colour, texture, movement, rhythm, melody, camerawork – although we are much less used to talking about them.

The nature of non-representational signs is not, however, so different from that of representational. Both are, in Peirce's terminology, largely iconic; but whereas the relationship between signifier and signified in a representational icon is one of resemblance between their appearance, their look, the relationship in the case of the non-representational icon is one of resemblance at the level of basic structuration.

This concept has been developed (among other places) in the work of Susanne K. Langer, particularly in relation to music. We are moved by music, yet it has the least obvious reference to 'reality' – the intensity of our response to it can only be accounted for by the way music, abstract, formal though it is, still embodies feeling.

> The tonal structures we call 'music' bear a close logical similarity to the forms of human feeling – forms of growth and of attenuation, flowing and stowing, conflict and resolution, speed, arrest, terrific excitement, calm or subtle activation or dreamy lapses – not joy and sorrow perhaps, but the poignancy of both – the greatness and brevity and eternal passing of everything vitally felt. Such is the pattern, or logical form, of sentience; and the pattern of music is that same form worked out in pure measures, sound and silence. Music is a tonal analogue of emotive life.
>
> Such formal analogy, or congruence of logical structures, is the prime requisite for the relation between a symbol and whatever it is to mean. The symbol and the object symbolized must have some common logical form.
>
> (Langer 1953: 27)

Langer realizes that recognition of a common logical form between a performance sign and what it signifies is not always easy or natural: 'The congruence of two given perceptible forms is not always evident upon simple inspection. The common *logical* form they both exhibit may become apparent only when you know the principle whereby to relate them' (ibid.). This implies that responding to a performance is not spontaneous – you have to learn what emotion is embodied before you can respond to it. A problem with this as Langer develops it is the implication that the emotion itself is not coded, is simply 'human feeling'. I would be inclined, however, to see almost as much coding in the emotions as in the signs for them. Thus, just as writers such as E. H. Gombrich and Umberto Eco stress that different modes of representation (in history and culture) correspond to different modes of perception, so it is important to grasp that modes of experiential art and entertainment correspond to different culturally and historically determined sensibilities.

This becomes clear when one examines how entertainment forms come to have the emotional signification they do: that is, by acquiring their signification in relation to the complex of meanings in the social-

Table 3.1

	Energy	*Abundance*
	Capacity to act vigorously; human power, activity, potential	Conquest of scarcity; having enough to spare without sense of poverty of others; enjoyment of sensuous material reality
Show-biz forms	Dance – tap, Latin-American, American Theater Ballet; also 'oomph', 'pow', 'bezazz' – qualities of performance	Spectacle; Ziegfeld, Busby Berkeley, MGM
Sources of show-biz forms	Tap – black and white folk culture; American Theater Ballet – modern dance plus folk dance plus classical ballet	Court displays; high art influences on Ziegfeld, Cedric Gibbons (MGM); *haute couture*
Golddiggers of 1933	'Pettin' in the Park' (tap, roller skates; quick tempo at which events are strung together)	'Pettin' . . .' (leisure park) 'We're in the Money' (showgirls dressed in coins) 'Shadow Waltz' (lavish sets; tactile, non-functional, wasteful clothing; violins as icon of high culture, i.e. expense)
Funny Face	'Think Pink' 'Clap Yo' Hands' (tap) 'Let's Kiss and Make Up' (tap, and Astaire's longevity) Cellar dance	'Think Pink' (use of materials and fabrics) 'Bonjour Paris' 'On How to be Lovely' (creation of fashion image)
On the Town	'New York, New York' 'On the Town' 'Prehistoric Man' 'Come up to My Place'	'New York, New York' (cf. 'Bonjour Paris') 'Miss Turnstiles' (woman as commodity-fantasy)
Westerns	Chases, fights, bar-room brawls; pounding music (1960s onwards)	Land – boundlessness and/ or fertility
TV news	Speed of series of sharp, short items; the 'latest' news; hand-held camera	Technology of news-gathering – satellites, etc.; doings of rich; spectacles of pageantry and destruction

Intensity	Transparency	Community
Experiencing of emotion directly, fully, unambiguously, 'authentically', without holding back	A quality of relationships – between represented characters (e.g. true love), between performer and audience ('sincerity')	Togetherness, sense of belonging, network of phatic relationships (i.e. those in which communication is for its own sake rather than for its message)
'Incandescent' star performers (Garland, Bassey, Streisand); torch singing	'Sincere' stars (Crosby, Gracie Fields); love and romance	The singalong chorus numbers
Star phenomenon in wider society; the Blues	Star phenomenon in wider society; eighteenth-century sentimental novel	Pub entertainment *and* parlour balladry; choral traditions in folk and church
'Forgotten Man' 'I've Got to Sing a Torch Song' (Blues inflections)	'Shadow Waltz' (Keeler and Powell as couple in eye-to-eye contact).	Showgirls (wise-cracking interaction, mutual support – e.g. sharing clothes)
'How Long Has This Been Going On?'	'Funny Face' 'He Loves and She Loves' ''S Wonderful'	(?) Cellar dance
'A Day in New York' ballet; climactic chase	'You're Awful' (insult turned into declaration of love) 'Come up to My Place' (direct invitation)	'You Can Count on Me'
Confrontation on street; suspense	Cowboy as 'man' – straight, straightforward, morally unambiguous, puts actions where his words are	Townships; cowboy camaraderie
Emphasis on violence, dramatic incident; selection of visuals with eye to climactic moments	(?) 'Man of the people' manner of some newscasters, celebrities and politicians (?) simplification of events to allow easy comprehension	The world rendered as global village; assumptions of consensus

cultural situation in which they are produced. Take the extremely complex history of tap dance – in black culture, tap dance has had an improvisatory, self-expressive function similar to that in jazz; in minstrelsy, it took on an aspect of jolly mindlessness, inane good humour, in accord with minstrelsy's image of the Negro; in vaudeville, elements of mechanical skill, tap dance as a feat, were stressed as part of vaudeville's celebration of the machine and the brilliant performer. Clearly there are connections between these different significations, and there are residues of all of them in tap as used in films, television and contemporary theatre shows. This has little to do, however, with the intrinsic meanings of hard, short, percussive, syncopated sounds arranged in patterns and produced by the movement of feet, and everything to do with the significance such sounds acquire from their place within the network of signs in a given culture at a given point of time. Nevertheless, the signification is essentially apprehended through the coded non-representational form (although the representational elements usually present in a performance sign – a dancer is always 'a person dancing' – may help to anchor the necessarily more fluid signification of the non-representational elements; for example, a black man, a white man in blackface, a troupe, or a white woman tap-dancing may suggest different ways of reading the taps, because each relates to a slightly different moment in the evolution of the non-representational form, tap dance).

I have laboured this point at greater length than may seem warranted partly with polemic intent. First, it seems to me that the reading of non-representational signs in the cinema is particularly undeveloped. On the one hand, the *mise-en-scène* approach (at least as classically developed in *Movie*) tends to treat the non-representational as a function of the representational, simply a way of bringing out, emphasizing, aspects of plot, character, situation, without signification in their own right. On the other hand, semiotics has been concerned with the codification of the representational. Second, I feel that film analysis remains notoriously non-historical, except in rather lumbering, simplistic ways. My adaptation of Langer seeks to emphasize not the connection between signs and historical events, personages, or forces, but rather the history of signs themselves as they are produced in culture and history. Nowhere here has it been possible to reproduce the detail of any sign's history (and I admit to speculation in some instances), but most of the assertions are based on more thorough research, and even where they are not, they should be.

The categories of entertainment's utopian sensibility are sketched in the accompanying Table 3.1, together with examples of them. The three films used will be discussed below; the examples from Westerns and television news are just to suggest how the categories may have wider application; the sources referred to are the cultural, historical situation of the code's production.

The categories are, I hope, clear enough, but a little more needs to be said about 'intensity'. It is hard to find a word that quite gets what I mean. What I have in mind is the capacity of entertainment to present either complex or unpleasant feelings (e.g. involvement in personal or political events; jealousy, loss of love, defeat) in a way that makes them seem uncomplicated, direct and vivid, not 'qualified' or 'ambiguous' as day-to-day life makes them, and without intimations of self-deception and pretence. (Both intensity and transparency can be related to wider themes in the culture, as 'authenticity' and 'sincerity' respectively – see Trilling 1972.)

The obvious problem raised by this breakdown of the utopian sensibility is where these categories come from. One answer, at a very broad level, might be that they are a continuation of the utopian tradition in western thought. George Kateb describes what he takes to be the dominant motifs in this tradition, and they do broadly overlap with those outlined above. Thus:

> when a man [sic] thinks of perfection . . . he thinks of a world permanently without strife, poverty, constraint, stultifying labour, irrational authority, sensual deprivation . . . peace, abundance, leisure, equality, consonance of men and their environment.
>
> (1972: 9)

We may agree that notions in this broad conceptual area are common throughout western thought, giving it, and its history, its characteristic dynamic, its sense of moving beyond what is to what ought to be or what we want to be. However, the very broadness, and looseness, of this common ground does not get us very far – we need to examine the specificity of entertainment's utopia.

One way of doing so is to see the categories of the sensibility as temporary answers to the inadequacies of the society which is being escaped from through entertainment. This is proposed by Hans Magnus Enzensberger in his 'Constituents of a theory of the media'. He takes issue with the traditional left-wing use of concepts of 'manipulation' and 'false needs' in relation to the mass media:

> The electronic media do not owe their irresistible power to any sleight-of-hand but to the elemental power of deep social needs which come through even in the present depraved form of these media.
>
> (1972: 113)

Consumption as spectacle contains the promise that want will disappear. The deceptive, brutal and obscene features of this festival derive from the fact that there can be no question of a real fulfilment of its promise. But so long as scarcity holds sway, use-value remains a decisive category which can only be abolished by trickery. Yet trickery on such a scale is only conceivable if it is based on mass need. This need – it is a utopian one – is there. It is the desire for a new ecology, for a breaking-down of environmental barriers, for an aesthetic which is not limited to the sphere of the 'artistic'. These desires are not – or are not primarily – internalized rules of the games as played by the capitalist system. They have physiological roots and can no longer be suppressed. Consumption as spectacle is – in parody form – the anticipation of a utopian situation.

(ibid.: 114)

This does, I think, express well the complexity of the situation. However, Enzensberger's appeal to 'elemental' and 'physiological' demands, although we do not need to be too frightened by them, is lacking in both historical and anthropological perspectives. I would rather suggest, a little over-schematically, that the categories of the utopian sensibility are related to specific inadequacies in society. I illustrate this in Table 3.2.

Table 3.2

Social tension/inadequacy/absence	Utopian solution
Scarcity (actual poverty in the society; poverty observable in the surrounding societies, e.g. Third World); unequal distribution of wealth	Abundance (elimination of poverty for self and others; equal distribution of wealth)
Exhaustion (work as a grind, alienated labour, pressures of urban life)	Energy (work and play synonymous), city-dominated (*On the Town*) or pastoral return (*The Sound of Music*)
Dreariness (monotony, predictability, instrumentality of the daily round)	Intensity (excitement, drama, affectivity of living)
Manipulation (advertising, bourgeois democracy, sex roles)	Transparency (open, spontaneous, honest communications and relationships)
Fragmentation (job mobility, rehousing and development, high-rise flats, legislation against collective action)	Community (all together in one place, communal interests, collective activity)

The advantage of this analysis is that it does offer some explanation of why entertainment *works*. It is not just left-overs from history, it is not *just* what show business, or 'they', force on the rest of us, it is not simply the expression of eternal needs – it responds to real needs *created by society*. The weakness of the analysis (and this holds true for

Enzensberger too) is in the give-away absences from the left-hand column – no mention of class, race, or patriarchy. That is, while entertainment is responding to needs that are real, at the same time it is also defining and delimiting what constitute the legitimate needs of people in this society.

I am not trying to recoup here the false needs argument – we are talking about real needs created by real inadequacies, but they are not the only needs and inadequacies of the society. Yet entertainment, by so orienting itself to them, effectively denies the legitimacy of other needs and inadequacies, and especially of class, patriarchal and sexual struggles. (Though once again we have to admit the complexity and contradictions of the situation – that, for instance, entertainment is not the only agency which defines legitimate needs, and that the actual role of women, gay men and blacks in the creation of show business leaves its mark in such central oppositional icons as, respectively, the strong woman type, e.g. Ethel Merman, Judy Garland, Elsie Tanner, camp humour and sensuous taste in dress and decor, and almost all aspects of dance and music. Class, it will be noted, is still nowhere.)

Class, race and sexual caste are denied validity as problems by the dominant (bourgeois, white, male) ideology of society. We should not expect show business to be markedly different. However, there is one further turn of the screw, and that is that, with the exception perhaps of community (the most directly working-class in source), the ideals of entertainment imply wants that capitalism itself promises to meet. Thus abundance becomes consumerism, energy and intensity personal freedom and individualism, and transparency freedom of speech. In other (Marcuse's) words, it is a partially 'one-dimensional' situation. The categories of the sensibility point to gaps or inadequacies in capitalism, but only those gaps or inadequacies that capitalism proposes itself to deal with. At our worse sense of it, entertainment provides alternatives *to* capitalism which will be provided *by* capitalism.

However, this one-dimensionality is seldom so hermetic, because of the deeply contradictory nature of entertainment forms. In Variety, the essential contradiction is between comedy and music turns; in musicals, it is between the narrative and the numbers. Both these contradictions can be rendered as one between the heavily representational and verisimilitudinous (pointing to the way the world is, drawing on the audience's concrete experience of the world) and the heavily non-representational and 'unreal' (pointing to how things could be better). In musicals, contradiction is also to be found at two other levels – within numbers, between the representational and the non-representational, and within the non-representational, due to the differing sources of production inscribed in the signs.

To be effective, the utopian sensibility has to take off from the real experiences of the audience. Yet to do this, to draw attention to the gap between what is and what could be, is, ideologically speaking, playing with fire. What musicals have to do, then, (not through any conspiratorial intent, but because it is always easier to take the line of least resistance, i.e. to fit in with prevailing norms) is to work through these contradictions at all levels in such a way as to 'manage' them, to make them seem to disappear. They don't always succeed.

I have chosen three musicals (*Golddiggers of 1933, Funny Face, On the Town*) which seem to me to illustrate the three broad tendencies of musicals – those that keep narrative and number clearly separated (most typically, the backstage musical); those that retain the division between narrative as problems and numbers as escape, but try to 'integrate' the numbers by a whole set of papering-over-the-cracks devices (e.g. the well-known 'cue for a song'); and those which try to dissolve the distinction between narrative and numbers, thus implying that the world of the narrative is also (already) utopian.

The clear separation of numbers and narrative in *Golddiggers of 1933* is broadly in line with a 'realist' aesthetic: the numbers occur in the film in the same way as they occur in life, that is, on stages and in cabarets. This 'realism' is of course reinforced by the social-realist orientation of the narrative, settings and characterization, with their emphasis on the Depression, poverty, the quest for capital, 'golddigging' (and prostitution). However, the numbers are not wholly contained by this realist aesthetic – the way in which they are opened out, in scale and in cinematic treatment (overhead shots, etc.) represents a quite marked shift from the real to the non-real, and from the largely representational to the largely non-representational (sometimes to the point of almost complete abstraction) (Figure 3.1). The thrust of the narrative is towards seeing the show as a 'solution' to the personal, Depression-induced problems of the characters; yet the non-realist presentation of the numbers makes it very hard to take this solution seriously. It is 'just' escape, 'merely' utopian.

If the numbers embody (capitalist) palliatives to the problems of the narrative – chiefly, abundance (spectacle) in place of poverty, and (non-efficacious) energy (chorines in self-enclosed patterns) in place of dis-spiritedness – then the actual mode of presentation undercuts this by denying it the validity of 'realism'.

However, if one then looks at the contradiction between the representational and non-representational within the numbers, this becomes less clear-cut. Here much of the representational level reprises the lessons of the narrative – above all, that women's only capital is their bodies as objects. The abundant scale of the numbers is an abundance of piles of women; the sensuous materialism is the texture of femaleness; the energy of the dancing (when it occurs) is the energy of the choreographic imagination, to which the dancers are subservient. Thus, while

Figure 3.1 Women as abundance: *Golddiggers of 1933*

the non-representational certainly suggests an alternative to the narrative, the representational merely reinforces the narrative (women as sexual coinage, women – and men – as expressions of the male producer).

Finally, if one then looks at the non-representational alone, contradictions once again become apparent – e.g. spectacle as materialism and metaphysics (that is, on the one hand, the sets, costumes, etc., are tactile, sensuous, physically exhilarating, but on the other hand, are associated with fairyland, magic, the by-definition immaterial), dance as human creative energy *and* sub-human mindlessness.

In *Funny Face*, the central contradiction is between art and entertainment, and this is further worked through in the antagonism between the central couple, Audrey Hepburn (art) and Fred Astaire (entertainment). The numbers are escapes from the problems, and discomforts, of the contradiction – either by asserting the unanswerably more pleasurable qualities of entertainment (e.g. 'Clap Yo' Hands' following the dirge-like Juliette Greco-type song in the 'empathicalist', i.e. existentialist, *soirée*), or in the transparency of love in the Hepburn–Astaire numbers.

But it is not always that neat: In the empathicalist cellar club, Hepburn escapes Astaire in a number with some of the other beats in the club. This reverses the escape direction of the rest of the film (i.e. it is an escape from entertainment/Astaire into art). Yet within the number, the contradiction repeats itself. Before Hepburn joins the group, they are dancing in a style deriving from Modern Dance, angular, oppositional shapes redolent in musical convention of neurosis and pretentiousness (cf. Danny Kaye's number, 'Choreography', in *White Christmas*). As the number proceeds, however, more show-biz elements are introduced – use of syncopated clapping, forming in a vaudeville line-up, and American Theater Ballet shapes. Here an 'art' form is taken over and infused with the values of entertainment. This is a contradiction between the representational (the dreary night club) and the non-representational (the oomph of music and movement), but also within the non-representational, between different dance forms. The contradiction between art and entertainment is thus repeated at each level.

In the love numbers, too, contradictions appear, partly by the continuation in them of troubling representational elements. In *Funny Face*, photographs of Hepburn as seen by Astaire, the fashion photographer, are projected on the wall as background to his wooing her and her giving in. Again, their final dance of reconciliation to ' 'S Wonderful' takes place in the grounds of a château, beneath the trees, with doves fluttering around them (Figure 3.2). Earlier, this setting was used as the finish for their fashion photography sequence. In other words, in both cases, she is reconciled to him only by capitulating to his definition of her (Figure 3.3). In itself, there is nothing contradictory in this – it is what Ginger Rogers always had to do. But here the mode of reconciliation is transparency and yet we can see the strings of the number being pulled. Thus the representational elements, which bespeak manipulation of romance, contradict the non-representational, which bespeak its transparency.

The two tendencies just discussed are far more common than the third, which has to suggest that utopia is implicit in the world of the narrative as well as in the world of the numbers.

The commonest procedure for doing this is removal of the whole film in time and space – to turn-of-the-century America (*Meet Me In St Louis*, *Hello Dolly!*), Europe (*The Merry Widow, Gigi, Song of Norway*), cockney London (*My Fair Lady, Oliver!, Scrooge*), black communities (*Hallelujah!*, *Cabin in the Sky, Porgy and Bess*), etc. – to places, that is, where it can be believed (by white urban Americans) that song and dance are 'in the air', built into the peasant/black culture and blood, or part of a more free-and-easy stage in American development. In these films, the introduction of any real narrative concerns is usually considerably delayed and comes chiefly as a temporary threat to utopia – thus reversing the other two patterns, where the narrative predominates and numbers function as temporary escapes from it. Not much happens, plot-wise, in *Meet Me in St Louis* until we have had 'Meet Me in St Louis', 'The Boy Next Door' 'The Trolley Song' and 'Skip to My Lou' – only then does father come along with his proposal to dismantle this utopia by his job mobility.

Most of the contradictions developed in these films are overridingly bought off by the nostalgia or primitivism which provides them with the point of departure. Far from pointing forwards, they point back, to a golden age – a reversal of utopianism that is only marginally offset by the narrative motive of recovery of utopia. What makes *On the Town* interesting is that its utopia is a well-known modern city. The film starts as an escape – from the confines of navy life into the freedom of New York, and also from the weariness of work, embodied in the docker's refrain, 'I feel like I'm not out of bed yet', into the energy of leisure, as the sailors leap into the city for their day off. This energy runs through the whole film, *including the narrative*. In most musicals, the narrative represents things as they are, to be escaped from. But most of the narrative of *On the Town* is about the transformation of New York into utopia. The sailors release the *social* frustrations of the women – a tired taxi driver just coming off shift, a hard-up dancer reduced to belly-dancing to pay for ballet lessons, a woman with a sexual appetite that is deemed improper – not so much through love and sex as through energy. This sense of the sailors as a transforming energy is heightened by the sense of pressure on the narrative movement suggested by the device of a time-check flashed on the screen intermittently.

Figure 3.2 The *mise-en-scène* of transparency: *Funny Face*

Figure 3.3 Constructing transparency: *Funny Face*

Figure 3.4   Energy from Ann Miller and primitivism: *On the Town*

This gives a historical dimension to a musical, that is, it shows people making utopia rather than just showing them from time to time finding themselves in it. But the people are men – it is still men making history, not men and women together. And the Lucy Schmeeler role is unforgivably male chauvinist. In this context, the 'Prehistoric Man' number is particularly interesting (Figure 3.4). It centres on Ann Miller, and she leads the others in the takeover of the museum. For a moment, then, a woman 'makes history'. But the whole number is riddled with contradictions, which revolve round the very problem of having an image of a woman acting historically. If we take the number and her part in it to pieces (Table 3.3), we can see that it plays on an opposition between self-willed and mindless modes of being; and this play is between representational (R) and non-representational (NR) at all aesthetic levels.

Table 3.3

Self-willed	Mindless
Miller as star (R)	Miller's image ('magnificent animal') (R)
Miller character–decision-maker in narrative (R)	Number set in anthropology museum – associations with primitivism (R)
Tap as self-expressive form (NR)	Tap as mindless repetitions (NR)
Improvisatory routine (R/NR)	

The idea of a historical utopianism in narrativity derives from the work of Ernest Bloch. According to Frederic Jameson, Bloch

> has essentially two different languages or terminological systems at his disposition to describe the formal nature of Utopian fulfilment: the movement of the world in time towards the future's ultimate moment, and the more spatial notion of that adequation of object to subject which must characterise that moment's content . . . [These] correspond to dramatic and lyrical modes of the presentation of not-yet-being.
>
> (1971: 146)

Musicals (and Variety) represent an extra ordinary mix of these two modes – the historicity of narrative and the lyricism of numbers. They have not often taken advantage of it, but the point is that they could, and that this possibility is always latent in them. They are a form we still need to look at if films are, in Brecht's words on the theatre, to 'organize the enjoyment of changing reality'.

NOTE

This chapter was originally published in spring 1977 in *Movie* 24.

REFERENCES

Enzensberger, Hans Magnus (1972) 'Constituents of a theory of the media', in Denis McQuail (ed.) *Sociology of Mass Communications*, Harmondsworth, Mx: Penguin, 99–116.
Jameson, Fredric (1971) *Marxism and Form*, Princeton, NJ: Princeton University Press.
Kateb, George (1972) *Utopia and its Enemies*, New York: Schocken.
Langer, Susanne K. (1953) *Feeling and Form*, London: Routledge & Kegan Paul.
Trilling, Lionel (1972) *Sincerity and Authenticity*, London: Oxford University Press.

FURTHER READING

Altman, Rick (ed.) (1981) *Genre: The Musical*, London: Routledge & Kegan Paul.
Altman, Rick (1987) *The American Film Musical*, Bloomington, Ind.: Indiana University Press.
Feuer, Jane (1982) *The Hollywood Musical*, London: Macmillan.
Gaines, Jane and Herzog, Charlotte (eds) (1990) *Fabrications: Costume and the Female Body*, London and New York: Routledge.
Geraghty, Christine (1991) *Women and Soap Opera*, Cambridge: Polity Press.
Lovell, Terry (1980) *Pictures of Reality*, London: British Film Institute.
Modleski, Tania (1982) *Loving with a Vengeance*, New York: Methuen.
Williams, Linda (1990) *Hard Core: the Frenzy of the Visible*, Berkeley, CA: University of California Press.

4 Quality pleasures

Rupert Murdoch putting the knife into 'quality drama' at the Edinburgh Television Festival is a bit of an embarrassment.[1] 'Qualities' have long been the bogeys of left criticism, their emotional restraint and good taste the embodiment of a middle-class, middle-aged, suburban sensibility, their period detail the televisual equivalent of the heritage industry, their overriding tones of regret and disappointment expended on the days of empire, classes in their place and servants always obtainable. It may not be Thatcherite television, too sad, uncertain and backward-looking for that, but it does comfort the middle classes with the proposition that however nice their homes and clothes, they do suffer a lot and it's hard to know anyway what's right and what's wrong, everything is so nuanced and 'difficult'.

Qualities are often both snobbish and complacent. The knee-jerk approval they get from so many within the industry and from television critics is so insufferable that one could almost be grateful for Mr Murdoch's spade-calling, were it not for one's awareness of the incommensurably greater tide of snobbery and complacency in his empire. One of the problems of the knee-jerk approval ('the British do these things so well') is that it is usually couched in terms of the qualities being somehow better than other things on television. They are not, necessarily. They have their own pleasures, which are their own justification.

The idea that the qualities are supremely 'well done' does not really tell you what they are doing. The phrase echoes those characters in Barbara Pym novels who observe wistfully of women a little better off than they that what these women wear may not look much but is 'good'. The well-done-ness has to do with the provenance of the material, the attention to detail and finish in acting, costume and setting, and the slowish pace, where aspects of how the thing is done take precedence over rattling through the plot or celebrating vivid performance. There is a thickness of texture in the qualities, very different from most soaps or US teledramas, where milieu and income are signalled through the selection of a few opulently designed or highly suggestive items of dress and décor.

The pleasure of this well-done density is partly sensuous – *Fortunes of War* would have been worth it for Harriet's cardigans and tea-cups alone (Figure 4.1); or, as a friend of mine puts it, the only trouble with qualities is that the actors will keep standing in front of the furniture. It is sensuousness in a particular register. Although the qualities are un- doubtedly very expensive, and most viewers know it, they are rarely set in worlds of the most extravagant or fashionable luxury. While most people could not afford to live as the characters in qualities do, it is just about possible to imagine being able to. Moreover, the detail and finish provide a pleasure akin to that taken by all enthusiasts of crafts, not least ones widely practised like carpentry, knitting, cooking, gardening. There is a relish and delight to be had from recognizing the skill and care that go into the qualities.

All of this well-done sensuousness is lavished on characters, settings and situations that are overridingly domestic and local. Qualities are therefore sometimes characterized, pejoratively, as 'superior soaps'. There would be nothing wrong with them if this were so (whatever it means), but in fact it misses what is specific to them.

In the qualities there are two countervailing tendencies. On the one hand, there is a strong feeling that the characters and what is happening to them are not really where it's at, a feeling of which they are often acutely aware. There are often offscreen, as crucial reference points, momentous world-historical events taking place: the end of the British Empire in India, the rise of fascism and the Second World War, the growth and decline of the welfare state in Britain, and so on. The characters, especially but not only the women, are aware of what's going on, but feel unable to affect or comprehend it – hence the mood of bafflement and melancholy, the strong sense of stasis rather than dy- namic plot development. Nothing could be more unlike soap operas. With them, home and community are where it's at, plots are squan- dered with astounding largesse. There may be recognition of 'wider' realms and events, but they are marginal to the real business of family, friends, day-to-day life. Soaps and the qualities may both favour the domestic, local world – the world of affect – but for the former that is also the centre of the world at large whereas for the qualities it is the margin.

On the other hand, the wider world does suddenly, distressingly, erupt into these margins. Wartime settings achieve this with the greatest of ease: arbitrary, unforeseeable, often gruesome deaths and maimings interrupt the round of perplexed marginality. This does not pull the characters to the centre of the world – it shatters the cosy safety of their lives while still reinforcing that sense of confusion and helplessness that is the qualities' abiding tone.

Soaps affirm and validate the importance of the immediate and the everyday, while the qualities give recognition to another, surely equally

Figure 4.1 Fortunes of War: Harriet and cardigan

Figure 4.2 The Jewel in the Crown: awkwardness in empire

widespread, feeling, of events, decisions, power going on elsewhere, over there, beyond our control or comprehension, though not so far beyond as to be incapable of hurting us. Both such constructions of feeling have their appeals, their strengths and limitations. One is not better than another; both discourage any sense of or desire for empowerment in the worlds of work, politics and 'society'; both validate different notions of the place of the domestic and local in the world. We do not need to defend one (qualities and public service broadcasting) at the critical expense of the other (soaps and monopolized, deregulated broadcasting). It is clear, however, that public service broadcasting has a better record at providing both. Certainly compared to Mr Murdoch.

NOTE

This chapter was originally published on 1 September 1989 in *New Statesman and Society*.

1 In 1989 Rupert Murdoch, the owner of huge private press and broadcasting systems, gave a key-note speech at the Edinburgh International Television Festival addressing the current debate over public broadcasting and castigating the latter's defenders for élitist

championing of documentary and literary adaptations. This occasioned the commissioning of this article.

FURTHER READING

Brunsdon, Charlotte (1990) 'Problems with quality', *Screen* 31 (1): 67–90.
Geraghty, Christine (1991) *Women and Soap Opera*, Cambridge: Polity Press.
Wollen, Tana (1991) 'Over our shoulders: nostalgic screen fictions for the 1980s', in John Corner and Sylvia Harvey (eds) *Enterprise and Heritage: Crosscurrents of National Culture*, London: Routledge, 178–93.

5 Classical ballet: a bit of uplift

The first time I saw Margot Fonteyn I was won over to classical ballet. I only ever saw her once live, from the very back of the next-to-highest level of Covent Garden. It was very hot and the stage was a very long way away. Rudolf Nureyev was in the show and seemed lazy and short on the anticipated smouldering sexuality. When Margot Fonteyn came on, I thought, Here we go with all that fiddling and fussiness. Then with a simple gesture of her right arm, unfolding out from the elbow, I got the point. That gesture literally embodied grace, poise, elegance, and in a way that transformed those qualities from empty routines learnt by upper-class girls in finishing schools to a dream of living in harmony with one's body.

This quality is at the heart of George Balanchine's choreography for the New York City Ballet. Most of his ballets dispense with story-line and subject-matter while often using difficult contemporary music. They are often spoken about as 'pure' dance, which is fine if you mean they are not 'about' anything in a philosophical sense, but not if you mean they are not expressive. The interplay of the dancers that creates patterns of charm and beauty depends on co-ordination and interdependence, moments of unity and moments of harmonious contrast, a sense of what it is like to interact, collectively to create something. The ballets are not 'about' collectivity, but they do show it, and show how beautiful it could feel.

Going to evening classes to learn classical ballet convinced me of the value of ballet. In my mid-thirties, I was one of the oldest people there and for most of the time the only man. I was stiff and uncoordinated. It was potentially embarrassing and humiliating. In fact it was wonderful. For me it was a revelation that I could feel elegant and graceful in my body, that movement need not just be good for me because it made me fit and strong, but because it made me feel good about my body. For my fellow women pupils, who had come, certainly, for the 'feminine' grace that classical ballet connotes, the exciting revelation was, on the contrary, precisely that feeling of stretch and strength in the muscles that is part of the pleasure of, for example, lifting weights.

Fonteyn, Balanchine, doing it – these are too inspiring, and too delightful, to be dismissed. Classical ballet celebrates the potential harmony of the human body, the utopian ideal of collective endeavour, the possibility of the interchange between the sexes of human qualities we now label masculine or feminine. Something of this is what has recommended ballet to the communisms of the USSR, Cuba and China. Beneath the aristocratic tat of the settings and the charming but dispensable never-never of the stories, there is an implicitly socialist vision.

Yet classical ballet must of course always come wrapped in the specifics of where and for whom it is performed, what other values and meanings it is attached to, and these are riven with contradictions. In practice, in Britain, classical ballet is, at one and the same time, élitist *and* popular, patriarchal *and* woman-centred, heterosexist *and* part of gay male culture, universal *and* distinctly white. It is all of this at once.

It is élitist in part because it is expensive. Not only are sets on a grand scale and not only do most of the classics require large casts, but behind all that there are the years of investment in training. Even a solo ballerina on a bare stage is the culmination of years of support and tuition. This élitism of money cuts two ways: those who get to be professional ballet dancers are the product of a rigorous process of selection; the high cost of putting on ballet means that there is not much of the live stuff about, to get in you have to be either wealthy or in the know. The symbol of classical ballet's élitism is Covent Garden, with its awe-inspiring entrance and studiedly dressed-down clientele, the usual story of the middle and upper classes getting reduced what they paid full price for before.

Yet classical ballet is also very popular. What live stuff there is, is well attended. Figures for the six major dance companies (the Royal, Sadler's Wells, London Festival, Northern, Rambert and London Contemporary) were well over a million during the past year [1985], despite the fact that cuts in subsidy mean there have actually been fewer performances. These figures do not take account of the numerous smaller companies, visiting companies and amateur performances. But this is only the tip of the iceberg of ballet's presence in our culture. Christmas TV always includes at least a couple of full-length ballets; pantomimes and Variety shows invariably include some kind of ballet spot (the good fairy is always in tutu and on pointe).

Above all, as a form of dance to learn, classical ballet remains a favourite. In local authority evening classes, it is the classical classes that you have to rush for to make sure you can get into them, even though there are far more such classes than in contemporary dance. The suburbs still have a generous quota of ballet schools aimed at little girls who still look alarmingly like miniature Margot Fonteyns.

These little girls are learning a dance form to which women have until recently been central. All the most interesting steps and roles, all the glory of the standard repertoire, is with the women. Yet it is male choreographers who have designed these steps and roles and in the process have constructed an image of women as the epitome of delicacy, femininity at its most debilitating. Held aloft like feathers by the ballerinos, incarnating the souls of swans and sprites, billowing across the stage on tippy-toes – the image of women in classical ballet has often been decried in feminist analysis.

The reality of the production of this image is its own exact contrary – sinew and sweat, muscles and strength are the actual stock in trade of the female ballet dancer. There is often an emphasis in the coverage of men in ballet on how athletic it all is, how you have to be butch to be a male dancer. Fair enough, but so you do to be a female dancer. Classical ballet has been one of the few areas, until very recently, where women were encouraged, indeed required, to develop their muscles, stamina and power, yet all in the service of the opposite feminine ideal.

The image of woman as sprite is of a piece with the way classical ballet focuses on the perfect heterosexual couple. Why then the gay appeal? One cannot reduce the appeal of something to a particular audience to one factor alone. Some gay men have been balletomanes for everything from the fact of ballet's extreme escapism from an uncongenial world to its display of the male physique, and to its reputation as an area of employment in which gay men could be open and safe.

There is also something about ballet's image of heterosexuality that fits with other items popular in gay male circles. Heterosexuality in classical ballet is so extreme, so refined, so ethereally idealized that it becomes rather unreal, a chimera. In a camp appreciation, this means enjoying the spectacle of heterosexuality paraded as glittering illusion. In a more aestheticized appreciation, the very abstraction of love in ballet renders it a kind of essence, not about women and men, nor about real people even, but the embodiment of an idea of human relationships that anyone can relate to.

Classical ballet yearns towards the potentials of the human body, all human bodies, stripped of the specifics of class, gender and sexuality. Yet there is also something distinctly white about ballet in Great Britain. In the USA, many of the top classical dancers are black, but not here. Perhaps this has been due to recruitment problems in the past. It is only recently that black dance groups, having found a new confidence in black traditions of dance, are turning to classical technique to extend their range. Yet there is also a racism among balletomanes. There lingers a view of the 'primitivism' of black people and their cultural traditions which is at odds with the ideas of poise and elegance so prized in classical ballet. But, if we look to the US traditions, we can see how the involvement of black dancers has enriched and inflected the classical image so that it becomes an affirmation of the way that, racially speaking, all kinds of body are graceful and powerful, vital and beautiful.

No art is truly universal, truly all-inclusive. Ballet does not accommodate disabled bodies and, as performers though not as participants, is unlikely to celebrate old or fat bodies. At one level, its yearning for the transcendent grace of the individual human body in the abstract is a refusal of the actual limitations of the human body in reality. But at another level, its dream of being at one with one's body and of being in harmony (united in and through differences) with other bodies is the feeling form of socialism. And the fact that you have to train and work for this is what makes it most powerful of all. Classical ballet does not say harmony is natural to human beings, but rather that we can learn to achieve it. Likewise, socialism does not emanate from us naturally, it is the harmony we can learn to create together.

NOTE

This chapter was originally published in *Marxism Today* in January 1986.

FURTHER READING

Daly, Ann (1987) 'The Balanchine woman', *The Drama Review* 113: 8–21.
Kealiinohomoku, Joann (1983) 'An anthropologist looks at ballet as a form of ethnic dance', in Roger Copeland and Selma Jean Cohen (eds) *What is Dance?*, Oxford: Oxford University Press.
McRobbie, Angela (1990) '*Fame, Flashdance* and fantasies of achievement', in Jane Gaines and Charlotte Herzog (eds) *Fabrications: Costume and the Female Body*, New York and London: Routledge, 3–58.

6 *The Sound of Music*

This is an attempt at a cultural reading of *The Sound of Music*. It is ideological in two senses. First, it is neither science nor simple subjectivism. It does not produce unquestionable, definitive knowledge or Truth (as is claimed – wrongly – for the natural sciences, and religion), but nor is it just what I happen to think. Rather it applies, openly and recognizably, an ideological position to the reading of the film (whilst not ignoring the question of evidence). This position places the reading within a developed, available intellectual and political debate – something fundamentally different from both 'value-free' science and the elaboration of personal taste or morality. Second, it is concerned with the way the ideology of the dominant groups in our society (above all, the bourgeoisie and men) operates in and on the film.

My argument is that in the case of *The Sound of Music*, the film sets up human (but also specifically female) problems, and solutions to them, that by implication run counter to the interests, and hence ideology, of the dominant groups. The film attempts to recoup this through various narrative and musical procedures (not through the conscious or conspiratorial intervention of the ruling groups, but because it is always more comfortable to fit in with dominant ideology – entertainment always seeks a point of comfort, whatever its point of departure). It seems likely that this pattern is very typical of Hollywood cinema, and perhaps especially of its supremely successful films.

Following the classic pattern of the musical, *The Sound of Music* is a movement between the narrative (in which problems, tensions and contradictions are set up) and the numbers (in which they are resolved or evaded). The narrative works chiefly, but not exclusively, through its representational, verisimilitudinous elements – the plot situations, the character types, the star images and so on. These are the elements people 'identify' with, and it is reasonable to hypothesize that the success of *The Sound of Music* is partly due to their managing to embody, dirndls notwithstanding, central problems and tensions in the lives of its predominantly female audience. In the case of the numbers, we have to pay more attention to the non-representational, sensuous-formal elements: music, movement, colour, texture and so on. These are not 'pure' or 'mere' forms, but rather embodiments of feeling. I follow here Susanne Langer's analysis of the artistic sign, whose meaning (or 'import' in her terminology) comes from the resemblance of the sign's shape and structure to the shape and structure of human feeling. Analysing the sensuous level of artistic signification means grasping the links between the formal, culturally developed rules of an artistic tradition (in this case, romantic popular music, Hollywood style, show-business traditions) and a sensibility which is crucially, but probably not wholly, determined by a specific culture. The tone and form of the numbers indicate, to use Raymond Williams's term, a culture's 'structure of feeling'. Both narrative and numbers, it should be stressed, are fields in which the dominant ideology may – and will always try to – operate, although the numbers especially tend to present themselves as pure realms of feeling, beyond ideology or even beyond culture.

WHAT HAPPENS

For anyone who has not seen the film recently (or at all), here is an outline of what happens in it, noting particularly where the numbers enter the narrative.

Section 1

Maria (Julie Andrews) sings 'The Sound of Music' on a hilltop. Peal of (we later learn) abbey bells sends her rushing off downhill. Credits sequence, with overture, including information that film is set in Salzburg 'in the last golden days of the 'thirties'. — Sung prayers in abbey ('*Dixit Dominus*', 'Allelujah'); several sisters complain ('Maria') to Mother Abbess (Peggy Wood) about novice Maria, who is late for prayers, bad-mannered and tactless; they are momentarily interrupted by Maria returning in haste from hills. — Mother Abbess advises Maria that spell in outside world might help her make up mind whether she really feels called to be nun; Maria sent to be governess to seven children of Captain von Trapp; leaving abbey Maria is nervous, but builds up courage by singing 'Confidence'. — Maria much impressed by beauty of von Trapp mansion, less impressed with Captain (Christopher Plummer) who orders home with severity, rules and regulations. — After dinner, eldest daughter Liesl (Charmian Carr) sneaks out of house to meet local delivery boy Rolf (Dan Truhitte) in grounds; 'You Are Sixteen'; they dance in summer-house as thunderstorm begins. — Liesl climbs back into house through Maria's bedroom window; they are joined by other children, frightened by thunder; Maria cheers them with 'My Favourite Things'; interrupted by Captain, appalled at singing; he also announces departure for Vienna next day. — Alone in room, Maria sings 'My Favourite Things' to self, leading to montage of Maria and children visiting Salzburg and playing; on hilltop, Maria gives them singing lesson, 'Do Re Mi'. — Captain returns with Baroness (Eleanor Parker) and Max (Richard Haydn), an impresario looking for folk acts for Salzburg festival; Captain shocked at appearance and liveliness of children, but Baroness charmed when they sing 'The Sound of Music' to her. — Maria and children put on puppet show for Captain and guests: 'The Lonely Goatherd'.

Section 2

After show, Liesl persuades Captain to sing; chooses 'Edelweiss'; Baroness silently observes Maria's attractiveness. – To please Baroness, Captain throws lavish ball; children and Maria watch from verandah; Maria teaches oldest boy Friedrich (Nicholas Hammond) the Ländler, an Austrian dance; half-way through Captain takes Friedrich's place, as Baroness watches; children say good-night in song, 'So Long, Farewell'; Baroness tells Maria Captain has fallen for her; anxious, Maria slips out of house. — Intermission. — Maria returns to abbey, where Mother Abbess tells her that she must not run away from problems but face them, 'Climb Every Mountain'. — Maria returns to von Trapp household in time to join in with children singing, rather lugubriously, 'My Favourite Things'. — Marriage of Baroness and Captain announced, but Baroness realizes where Captain's feelings really are, and regretfully sends him out into grounds where Maria is wandering; in summerhouse they express love, 'Something Good'. — Spectacular wedding scene: 'Maria' integrated with organ processional hymn.

Section 3

Returning from honeymoon, Captain and Maria find Max has entered children in festival; Captain forbids it, but when realizes life and family threatened by Nazis, consents to appearing with children and Maria in attempt to foil Nazis. — Under cover of festival, where they're awarded first prize, they escape, hiding for moment in abbey, over mountains to Switzerland ('Climb Every Mountain' over).

SECTION 1

The first part of *The Sound of Music*, up to and including 'The Lonely Goatherd', is structured around an opposition, which is lived out as a conflict of feeling by the heroine, Maria. This opposition is between two realms of existence – the first, totalitarian, represented by the abbey and then by the von Trapp household; the second, free, spontaneous and experiential, embodied in the experience of music.

The two opening numbers of the film, 'The Sound of Music' and the abbey sequence (sung prayers, 'Maria') express the opposition clearly. The first sums up from the word go what music means for the heroine and the film. Music is identified with nature, nature as conceived by the Romantics. The camera takes us down from the cold, bare regions of the mountain-tops to the lush, green world of the hills. This is a natural world, but one into which humanity can fit harmoniously. It is the fulfilment of the promise of the background music, affirming that the hills are indeed not just accompanied by music but alive with it. The lyrics of the song pick on close detail, where a natural sound translates to a musical or human one, and where the dynamics of this sound correspond to the dynamics of human feeling:

> My HEART wants to *beat like* the wings of a *bird* that flies from the
>   lake to the trees,
> To SIGH *like* a chime from a *bell* that flies from the church on a
>   *breeze*,
> To LAUGH *like* a *brook* as it leaps and falls over stones on its way,
> To *sing* through the night *like* a *lark* that is learning to PRAY.

The last line draws attention to a further affirmation of the song, that the music of nature is a form of religious experience, but not so much Christian as direct contact with the essential and the everlasting:

> The hills fill my heart with the sound of music,
> With songs they have heard *for a thousand years* . . .
> My heart will be *blessed* with the sound of music
> And I'll sing once more.

The import of this song – the innate musicality of nature, Maria's identification with it, its ability to inspire her to song – is underlined by cutting from Maria on the hilltop to her wandering among trees, along a brook, or picked out against the sky in the final affirmation (the last two lines quoted above).

This 'free' editing (following the logic of the song, not geography) combines with the sweeping camerawork, the full-bodied singing and the wide open spaces to define music as spontaneity, freedom, the untrammelled outpouring of pure feeling. In this, *The Sound of Music* is drawing on conceptions of music widespread in our culture. It is very commonly believed that music is a pure realm of feeling, beyond ideology. Here ideology is identified with politics, business, advertising, the rat race – realms of manipulation, alienation, unfreedom. This definition of music in a sense precludes any understanding of a positive, participatory, non-alienative ideology by pointing to an absolute, nature-music, that is beyond any imaginable culture or society. It is a measure of the sense of manipulation and alienation among people in this society that, quite by accident no doubt, in one of its most popular films the ideal identified as the non-ideological is so insistently evoked.

By contrast with this sequence, the musical world of the abbey is ordered, ritual, formal. After the sweeping camera and free editing of 'The Sound of Music', the '*Dixit Dominus*' is static, measured. Each shot is carefully composed, with balanced lighting, still camera. A sequence of close-ups of nuns at prayer emphasizes the conventionality of this world – there are either the young, fresh, innocent faces of novices, clean and scrubbed and healthy, or the older, lined, wise yet still innocent faces of the higher orders. We see no one middle-aged or ugly. Again, during the song 'Maria', the camera remains static, and formal composition of groups of nuns standing in the courtyard is used throughout. The bounce of the tune is not reproduced by the staging, which remains rigid and formal. Before the last line of the song, Maria bursts into the abbey, hair tousled, not looking where she is going. The nuns look at her, then sing slowly, in 'reverent' harmony: 'How do you hold a moonbeam in your hand?' This catches exactly how Maria fits into their world – she cannot be pinned down, she shatters the style of abbey life and yet she is magical too, charming and indefinable. They feel the pull of 'music', just as she does.

Although there is music in the abbey, it represents an approach to life quite different from that shown in the opening sequence, and this approach is elaborated by what we learn of the abbey and Maria's inability to fit into its highly structured life. The rules, written and unwritten, of abbey life cramp Maria's style, stifle her musicality, seem to cut out the freedom that music asserts. She is unable to remember prayer times, to keep her mouth shut and stop arguing, and for much of the time this is played for laughs, as when Maria says of the sister who makes her kiss the floor after an argument: 'Now I kiss the floor when I see her coming to save time!' But Maria's attitude towards the abbey is ambivalent – vexing as life is there, she feels greatly drawn to it, not only because of the goodness of the nuns but because she was drawn to the abbey during her girlhood reveries on the mountains. Despite all its restrictions, there is something in the abbey that corresponds to what Maria finds in the hills. She too feels the pull of 'order'.

In the von Trapp household, the opposition is more stark – music and silence. Captain von Trapp has banned music, and most speech, from the house. He has organized the lives of the children and servants so rigidly that they answer to the call of a whistle and follow a strict pattern of daily life. The 'natural' bubbling spontaneity of the children has been systematically suppressed. It is against this totalitarian regime (Figure 6.1), iconographically summed up in the cold thin lips, acid blue eyes and militarily precise dress of Christopher Plummer's Captain von Trapp, that Maria must assert, with renewed force, her musicality.

At this stage in the film, Maria is attempting to make the world a

Figure 6.1 The Sound of Music: Captain von Trapp and the children

Figure 6.2 The Sound of Music: Maria and the children

world of music. This is expressed in the transition song from the abbey to the von Trapp household, 'Confidence'. The lyrics of the song express Maria's confidence in herself and in the world, her determination to show herself and the world what she can do. It is sung in a forceful manner, with a complete sureness of pitch and a confident breaking of the musical line (e.g. consider the way Julie Andrews turns the middle section almost into an harangue: 'Strength doesn't lie in wealth! Strength doesn't lie in wealth! Strength lies in nights of peaceful slumbers, when you wake up, get up! it's healthy!') Her movements are a determined stride forward and, towards the end, a leaping movement, clicking the heels together. In the length of the song Maria moves from the abbey to the von Trapp home – as in the journey number, 'Don't Rain on my Parade', in *Funny Girl*, the song remains intact while the stages of the journey are seen only briefly, edited together. Not only does the song remain intact, but whenever we see the heroine, no matter what stage of the journey she has reached, she is still singing the song and is at the right moment in the song. The action is telescoped to fit the song, the logic of the real world gives way to the logic of the song, of music. And as in *Funny Girl*, nothing could be more appropriate, for by it we see the world come under the control and determination of the heroine, whose very essence is music. In the rest of the first part of the film, which is incidentally the richest in musical numbers, the concepts lying behind the notion of 'music' are elaborated. Each number deepens the picture.

'My Favourite Things' is the occasion for the demonstration of music's power to banish the fears of the real world. The children have run to Maria's room, terrified by the thunderstorm. To cheer them up, she asks them to think of nice things like kittens, rainbows, snow, and out of the list develops the song. But it is essentially the *music* that cheers, not thinking of the nice things, for when, later in the film (after Maria has temporarily left the von Trapps), the children attempt to reprise the song, the result is lugubrious, dispirited. It is only when Maria returns during the attempted reprise, and in her singing recovers the song's bounce, that it is effective. This is because 'My Favourite Things', despite its lyrics, expresses in the way it is presented more the essential spontaneity and warm community of music than the comfort of nice thoughts. As Maria lists the nice things, the inherent rhythm of the natural speech is picked up pizzicato on the strings, which thus lifts the list into the lilt of the song. The song develops 'spontaneously' from the natural rhythms of speech; music follows 'naturally' as the list calls forth joyfulness. The editing of the song is remarkable, for the sureness of touch with which one shot follows another (in the fairly small space of Maria's bedroom) gives the sense of the whole number being filmed continuously – as on live television, the performers sing and romp straight through the number, whilst the director cuts from camera to camera. Except that if you look closely, you see that it cannot possibly have been done like that, since there would be cameras in shot and a quite alarming number of them at that. But through the editing (the editor is William Reynolds and the director Robert Wise, who began his career as an editor), the perfect illusion is given of a spontaneously generated sense of togetherness being 'captured' by the camera.

'Do Re Mi' emphasizes first of all that it is singing itself which is fun. This is an extremely important point, for whilst the film certainly suggests varying ways in which music is important, it never allows it to be merely symbolic. Music does not 'stand for' other things, but is the locus of other values. It is crucial to assert the physical pleasure of music itself, the joy of singing in its own right. Hence the singing lesson concentrates on the notes and how to put them together, and not on what singing makes you feel or what you can express through it. Singing is *sui generis*. But, again, the staging presents a further dimension. It starts on a hilltop, much the same setting as for 'The Sound of Music', but as the number develops and the children pick up the notes and the melody, the song takes off into a sequence of shots in and around Salzburg (Figure 6.2), the children and Maria dancing along a river-bank, riding bicycles, imitating the poses of statues. Here again, this free editing, shaped by musical rather than real-world logic, conveys the extent to which music takes over the world – or feels as if it does to singers. The rhythms of the editing convey the dynamics of the experience as it feels to the participants.

'The Lonely Goatherd' is performed as a puppet show by Maria and the children to please the Captain and the Baroness. The puppets act out a story which is just hinted at in the song's lyrics – a red-cheeked, dopey-looking boy is bashful with a pretty, long-eyelashed girl; her mother 'with a gleaming gloat' pushes her into the boy's arms, the prelude to their marriage and happiness. The story is re-enacted by a pair of goats (the female again having long eyelashes) and their story rounds off with two baby goats.

Much of 'The Lonely Goatherd' expresses again the sheer pleasure of making music. For much of the time the song is not saddled with a lyric at all, but simply consists of yodelling, the pure joy of musical utterance. This occurs, however, within a context which is of some interest: it is the context of a complete certainty about the nature of the world, or, to be more specific, the context of a firmly held common-sense view of sexual relationships. This view has two central points – the difference between the sexes and the manner by which marriage is achieved.

In 'The Lonely Goatherd', there is no problem about knowing what the difference between the sexes is (over and above the obvious physical differences). The images of the goatherd and the girl express in grotesque miniature a certainty which is expressed elsewhere in the film – for instance, when Maria pleads with von Trapp on behalf of his children:

each one is presented as having a specific need for the Captain, based not on his or her individuality, but on their sex and the stage they have reached. Thus the eldest girl, being at that age and being a girl, needs freedom to have boyfriends without losing the assurance that her father still cares; the eldest boy, just at the turn of adolescence, needs to feel his father's support but – 'of course' – is too proud to show it; and so on, down to the youngest child, too little a person to want anything but 'just to love you'. People are transparent, sex and age determinant.

Equally certain in the antics of the puppets is the view that life is structured around female manipulation of the male, through prettiness in youth and domination in middle-age. To some extent both this and the view of sexual differences are borne out by subsidiary characters and scenes in the film – the children are not developed much as individuals; the Baroness is most adept at 'handling' von Trapp whilst Max Detweiler is weak and venial; there is irony in the scene between Rolf and Liesl, where he tells her to rely on him because he is 'older and wiser'. But, as we shall see, this certainty is not quite so firm in Maria and von Trapp as the film develops.

'The Sound of Music', 'My Favourite Things', 'Do Re Mi' and 'The Lonely Goatherd', taken together, represent the realm of freedom and joy, of music, as against the formality and restrictions of the abbey and the silence and rigidity of the von Trapp household. A further dimension to this opposition, not expressed directly in music, is that of class. Maria is of peasant origins, a fact that the film stresses. It gives a further validity to her spontaneous musicality, for it implies her uncomplicated closeness to the sources of music, nature and herself. The rudeness of peasant ways, the lack of circumspection and tact may also be what upset the well-spoken sisters who complain of her to the mother Abbess. When she arrives at the von Trapp mansion she is daunted but refuses to be over-impressed (as conveyed in Julie Andrews's performance); left alone in a great hall, she mocks aristocratic ways by bowing low and obsequiously. She refuses to let von Trapp's icy politeness freeze her out, doggedly speaks her mind and is not above sending him up. The spirit of peasant mockery of fine and fancy manners lingers in her. Yet she is also impressed by the grandeur of the household, the charm of the children, the name and tradition of the family. She may mock them, but she also respects them. She is pulled both ways.

JULIE ANDREWS

An important inflection of the freedom/order opposition is carried, as a kind of sub-text, in the image and performance of Julie Andrews.

The Andrews image, which for some people is a reason for not going to see *The Sound of Music*, is made up basically of her roles in this film, *Mary Poppins* and the stage version of *My Fair Lady*. All subsequent appearances have been an attempt to break away from it. These three early roles have much in common, and the clear, bell-like, middle-class tones and jolly, awkward stance for which Andrews is often derided, are especially appropriate to them.

In terms of class, she plays characters of indeterminate or dubious class origin and ambiguous present position. In *My Fair Lady* she was archetypically a cockney lass. As Mary Poppins she was magic in origin – floating down from the sky, using an umbrella as a parachute. And Maria is a peasant girl, although peasant is a somewhat vague term, giving us no indication of wealth or occupation (farm labourer, tenant farmer, market gardener?). Maria's background is in fact still more indefinite by virtue of being an orphan, and then a novice. Each character enters a distinctly upper-class world – Eliza Doolittle passes herself off as belonging to it, something achieved above all through linguistic mastery; Mary and Maria are in a more ambiguous position – they are governesses. This is at once a servant job and a middle-class profession, although in Maria's case this latter has little meaning – she has had no training, has no job aspirations, in no way 'belongs' to a group of people which might be termed a profession. In none of these roles does Julie Andrews embody a middle-class type or view of the world, although all three are people who have gained entry to and acceptance in the upper reaches of society (royalty in *My Fair Lady*, aristocracy in *The Sound of Music*, banking upper-middle-class in *Mary Poppins*). In these contexts, the crisp and absolute precision of Julie Andrews's delivery has a certain edge to it, for it is the character's chief hold on acceptance.

In terms of sexuality, neither Mary Poppins nor Maria is free, uninhibited, sensual, although Eliza (at any rate so the number 'Show Me!' suggests) very probably is. The chimney sweep (Dick Van Dyke) who is in love with Mary implies that she is sexually inadequate – unfeeling, unable to respond, stiff. Maria on the other hand retreats to the abbey as soon as she begins to feel drawn to the Captain. The feelings confuse her, disorient her – she lacks, as have women in this culture for over a century, any definition of or role for female sexuality. In this sense, then, Andrews's sexual awkwardness provides a kind of negative variation on the image of 'natural feeling' so positively affirmed in music. Once we have a definition of what freedom is like – here summed up in the numbers – we can embrace it joyously (hence the political importance of utopianism), but a freedom of feeling that knows no definition – as here with the female sexual impulse – is terrifying. Andrews as Maria *suffers* from just this aspect of the situation of women, and it provides a sombre possibility for audience identification that the film cannot really explore any further.

SECTION 2

The problems set up in the first part of the film are resolved in the second (i.e. from after 'The Lonely Goatherd' to the wedding of Maria and von Trapp) through the mediations of folk culture, and love and marriage. These represent the realization of Maria's aim – the unification of music and the world, of freedom and order.

Two of the turning-points in the narrative are based on folk culture – the song von Trapp is persuaded to sing, 'Edelweiss', and his dance, a Ländler, with Maria during the ball. The use of folk idioms, melodies, dance forms to enrich the dominant tradition of culture has long been part of musical history – the nationalist movement in music was fundamentally based on it – Grieg, Sibelius, Bartók, Dvořák, etc. – and the dance used here, the Ländler, is commonly supposed to have been the form from which the waltz was developed. Folk culture in this sense is the nexus of a form of nationalism, in which class distinctions melt and natural bonds are reasserted. The use of folk music, as opposed to the official written music, allows the dominant class to return to the people, to emphasize the common bond of a national heritage over and beyond present inequalities. Moreover, built into the idea of a return to the people is the idea of a return to nature, for the people, being less 'sophisticated', are held to be closer to nature and hence to the natural sources of music.

This is a romantic nationalism, basing itself in the culture of a peasantry declining in the face of industrialism and even in the qualities of the national geography (cf. *Song of Norway* where the music is shown to express the 'heart' of fjord scenery). It is also peculiarly apt, especially in musicals set in Europe, to unite the aristocracy and the peasantry, opposite but in some sense 'authentic' poles of the national culture, against the bureaucrats, the money-grubbers, or the spirit of the petty bourgeoisie incarnate in Nazism (cf. *Naughty Marietta, Call Me Madam, The Merry Widow, King's Rhapsody, Song of Norway*, etc.).

All this lies behind the use of respectable folk idioms in *The Sound of Music* – the song with its gentle, undemanding melody, its simple flower-as-emblem lyric; the dance, with its restrained formality and grace – as transition points for the breaking-down of the class barrier between Maria and the Captain, and in his conversion to music. Moreover, by introducing the nationalist element here, we are prepared for the final section of the film (the Germany/Austria confrontation).

Folk culture sets up a basis for understanding between Maria and von Trapp, but narrative expectations demand that this should issue in love and marriage. This duly happens, yet with an odd lack of conviction on the film's part, in the 'Something Good' number. This takes place in the summer-house, a setting already established as a locus of love by the number 'You Are Sixteen'. But where this number was bright and gay, culminating in a strutting and leaping dance choreographed to a thunderstorm and cymbal crashes, 'Something Good' is shot in misted focus, semi-darkness, with stillness of movement in both performers and camera. One could say it embodies the characters' uncertainty and caution, yet it also effectively blurs their interaction, as if Maria and von Trapp, and therefore freedom and order, are not, folk culture notwithstanding, really compatible. Thus the film manages to dissolve the contradictions and get us to the narrative resolution in marriage, but through the rather weak strategies of folk culture, a thinly realized love match and the spectacle of a wedding with baroque architecture and cathedral choir. Although the film now proceeds as if it had kicked over the trace of the earlier narrative tensions, they surface again, to be resolved only by the rather more stoic closing image.

SECTION 3

At this point, the film suddenly stops being a musical. There are no new numbers in the rest of the film, only reprises of 'Edelweiss' and 'Climb Every Mountain'. This is a pattern common in Rodgers and Hammerstein musicals: the climax of *The King and I* is the escape of Tup-Tim, her recapture, Anna's challenge to the King as he is about to whip the girl, and his collapse; the dénouement of *South Pacific* is a conventional war sequence, with one of the heroes bombed while on a spying mission. Similarly, *The Sound of Music* contains an exciting, but completely unmusical, climax of escape from Nazi patrols and over the border into Switzerland. What happens in each of these films is the growth and accomplishment of an understanding between the characters, which is then threatened by the intervention of a hostile country (Britain, Japan, Germany respectively) – the understanding is symbolized by an integration of music and narrative, so that the whole film becomes a musical world, which is then threatened and must be recovered by practical action. This narrative structure, with its strong emphasis on both interpersonal and patriotic loyalties, is in fact central to the intentions of Hammerstein, the librettist, who, as a member of the League of World Government, explicitly sought in the musicals to plead for tolerance towards other countries and their right to their own heritage and life-style (as expressed, of course, in their music or, ironically, Rodgers's Americanized version of it).

In the case of *The Sound of Music*, we have not only Germany threatening Austria, a straight nationalist threat, but another totalitarian regime, Nazism, which literally threatens musicality in its hostility to von Trapp's taking part in the Salzburg festival. But for this reworking of the freedom/order opposition, there is to be no magical resolution. The film ends with the family crossing the border over the mountains, the screen ringing with 'Climb Every Mountain'. This song was first introduced during Maria's temporary retreat to the abbey (where it is again shot with great formality, the Mother Abbess turning away into the shadow to begin it, and finally standing for the last verse with the stained-glass window lighting her beatifically). It fits in at the end in one sense simply because they are indeed climbing a mountain. Moreover, in its imagery the song takes up again the whole notion of human personality taking over nature, realizing the promise of background music. Facing up to life is seen as meeting the various obstacles that nature presents us with – mountains, streams, rainbows. . . . But by slipping into rainbow imagery, into the goal named as 'your dream', the song also hints at the fact that this is a never-ending quest, that life is a business of going on going on. And indeed this is where the film leaves it, not neat and tidy, for although the family has escaped the Germans, where have they really reached? We leave them climbing a mountain, not realizing a dream.

CONCLUSION

The Sound of Music takes as its point of departure real-life tensions, presented in an imaginative form – class relationships, sexual ambivalences and, centrally, the continuing contradiction between utter personal freedom and the social order of vested interests that is the enduring mark of bourgeois democracy. The film does not of course penetrate these contradictions to the realities of power and control, but rather presents the way the contradictions look and feel as they are lived. The film tries to offer easy ways out through the ideologies of nationalism and marriage, yet they are not brushed aside so lightly, and the film ends rather with a celebration of human endurance, the capacity to go on going on.

The Sound of Music takes this ending from both the musical and the 'woman's picture'. The happy ending commonly attributed to musicals is often, especially in later examples, of a fairly tough and bitter kind – think of *A Star is Born*, *Funny Girl*, *Gypsy*, *Sweet Charity*, *Cabaret*; and Rodgers and Hammerstein have made a feature of women's songs of endurance, self-sacrifice and hope – for instance, 'Climb Every Mountain', 'Something Wonderful' (*The King and I*), 'You'll Never Walk Alone' (*Carousel*), and, in lighter vein, 'A Cock-Eyed Optimist' (*South Pacific*). Similarly, the woman's picture, in its weepie form, begins from a presentation of the double bind that women in society are faced with: the systematically contradictory roles that a woman is expected to inhabit – siren, paragon of virtue; wife (partner), mother (authority) and servant (looking after men). One of the ways out of this is simply to celebrate the capacity of the heroine to carry on in this impossible position: the genteel ability to cope of Greer Garson in *Mrs Miniver*, the determination and endurance of Joan Crawford in *Mildred Pierce*, the matriarchal control and self-sacrifice of Irene Dunne in *I Remember Mama* and so on. In *Gone with the Wind*, two types of this capacity are represented: Vivien Leigh's Scarlett, wilfulness becoming mature will-power, and Olivia de Havilland's Melanie, patient and enduring.

With its stylistic oppositions of music/order, with the determination of 'Confidence', the ability to find pleasure in small things ('My Favourite Things') and with the message of 'Climb Every Mountain', *The Sound of Music* goes directly into a world where women are caught between asserted individuality and strong pressures on role conformity, where much pleasure must be invested in trivial items, and where the horizons are such as let only endurance, the ability to go on, make immediate sense as a life-project. The question is whether it simply celebrates these attitudes, hence giving them a much-needed recognition and symbolic form, or else also locks its female audience more inexorably into trivia and endurance. But the Endurance of the People is one of the great socialist themes, and I don't see why we should disparage it just because it is in *The Sound of Music*.

NOTE

This chapter was originally published in winter 1976–7 in *Movie* 23.

7 *Sweet Charity*

A standard model for the history of a genre could be divided into three periods: primitive, mature and decadent. The first shows the genre in embryonic form, the second the full realization of its expressive potential and the third a reflective self-consciousness about the genre itself. If there is anything in this at all, then *Sweet Charity* represents the supreme achievement of the musical in its decadent period. It uses every trick in the cinematic book to embody the musical qualities of rhythm, melody and tone, and uses its total visual, aural and choreographic musicality to express a cynically wise view of the limitations of the musical genre.

The director Bob Fosse makes full use of the musical qualities of film – the rhythmic potential of editing, the melodic sweep of camera movement, the orchestral flair of colour and design. The cuts in 'If My Friends Could See Me Now' follow precisely the line of the song; the exact timing of the camera dolly that opens 'I'm a Brass Band' visualizes the exultant speed of the music.

Sweet Charity is full of such intoxicating effects, and yet they all go to produce a critique of 'the musical' which more than anything else suggests the hollowness of the genre's gospel of happiness. The story of most musicals is the pursuit and achievement of happiness, and in the classic examples the numbers are moments when happiness is achieved. *Sweet Charity* also follows this narrative pattern. Charity's story is a series of episodes, each of them an encounter with a potential source of happiness. But each of these sources lets her down, and the treatment of happiness in the musical numbers already expresses the emptiness of what is on offer, even before Charity realizes it herself.

There are four major areas of potential happiness in Charity's story – religion, love, entertainment and friendship. Religion is dealt with in only one number, 'The Rhythm of Life', where the lyrics of Sammy Davis Jr's wicked performance as Big Daddy, the busy colours of the believers' clothes and their crazed, cramped body-movements all mercilessly mock that type of organized religion, especially in its trendier forms.

Love is dealt with more kindly, but no more credulously. Three

Figure 7.1 Sweet Charity: women for men

Figure 7.2 Sweet Charity: women for themselves

numbers mark Charity's relationship with Oscar: the first, 'It's a Nice Face', is half whispered to a prostrate Oscar after he has fainted in the lift – the feeling is very low-key; he sings the second, 'Sweet Charity' to her, their mutual exhilaration rendered 'unreal' by being shot in slow motion to emphasize what becomes evident immediately afterwards, that his love is based on his not knowing that she is a dance-hall hostess; and the third, Charity's 'I'm a Brass Band', sung when Oscar asks her to marry him despite what he now knows about her, is splendid but bizarre. Charity, dressed in a bright red uniform, dances around deserted New York streets like a majorette. She cries out 'Somebody loves me!' and a whole stadium of people roars approval. It is a delirium of love based, as is soon clear, on the quicksands of Oscar's hang-ups.

However, the most penetrating use of musical numbers is reserved for those set in places of entertainment – 'Big Spender' (Figure 7.1) in the dance-hall where Charity works, and the dances in the posh Pompeii club. Worlds apart socially, they are very similar choreographically – insistently sexual, yet in an angular, stiffened, ugly way that has nothing of sensuous enjoyment in it. 'If My Friends Could See Me Now' also refers to professional entertainment. Sung and danced by Charity, it expresses her jubilation at being in Vittorio Vitale's flat, and the musical form she instantly turns to is vaudeville, ending up with a spotlit hat-and-cane routine. She is really happy, but the movement is hectic, the cutting frantic, and in a final hallucinatory moment it is as if she is really on a stage – which is precisely how fragile her happiness is.

It is only with the treatment of friendship that the cynicism abates. The film only indicates *after* 'There's Gotta Be Something Better Than This' the futility of employment aspirations for hookers, and *after* 'I Love to Cry at Weddings' the futility of the institution of marriage. While they are on screen, both numbers feel straightforwardly happy. 'There's Gotta Be Something Better Than This' (Figure 7.2) uses a kind of vigorous movement more often associated with male dancers to express the solidarity and determination of the three women (MacLaine magnificently supported by Chita Rivera and Paula Kelly). 'I Love to Cry at Weddings' uses soft-shoe barbershop harmonies, streamers and confetti to evoke an old-fashioned community of well-wishing. Only with friends (not lovers), only where she works – the very places she so seldom really looks – are there glimmers of real happiness to be found.

NOTE

This chapter was originally published in 1981 in *The Movie* 75.

8 Four films of Lana Turner

Despite the enormous interest in stars, there has been very little study of them, and this has predominantly been sociological, concerned with how stars function in general ideological/cultural terms. Such concerns are certainly central to film studies, but we also need to know how stars function within the films themselves, that is, how the films articulate, carry, inflect, or subvert the general ideological/cultural functions. This article examines the way a single star image, Lana Turner's, is variously used in films in relation to other elements such as the construction of character, narrative, *mise-en-scène* and so on.[1]

Why Lana Turner? In part, certainly, because I like her; but her work also illustrates certain characteristic features of the star phenomenon. The four films discussed use her in different ways. In *Ziegfeld Girl*, the Turner image sends the film off-course and in effect partly cracks open its central mythology, whereas in *The Postman Always Rings Twice* (hereinafter, *Postman*) the image both holds together and exposes contradictory elements. *The Bad and the Beautiful* elaborates upon and finally celebrates the image, while *Imitation of Life* examines and scrutinizes it, holding it up to the light to expose it. More generally, Turner illustrates three of the ways that stars function *cinematically* (that is, within the total signifying practice of the cinema industry situated within society as a whole).

1 Her career is marked by an unusually, even spectacularly, high degree of interpenetration between her publicly available private life and her films. The star phenomenon depends upon collapsing the distinction between the star-as-person and the star-as-performer. This does not usually mean that the incidents of a film's scenario are taken to be actual incidents in the star's life but rather that they reveal or express the personality or type-of-person of the star. In the case of Turner, however, not only do her vehicles furnish characters and situations in accord with her off-screen image, but frequently incidents in them echo incidents in her life so that by the end of her career films like *Peyton Place*, *Imitation of Life*, *Madame X* and *Love Has Many Faces* seem in parts like mere illustrations of her life.

In the earlier films, Turner's image exemplifies one of the major forms of relationship between a star and her/his social context, namely the reconciliation of contradictions. Stars frequently speak to dominant contradictions in social life – experienced as conflicting demands, contrary expectations, irreconcilable but equally held values – in such a way as to appear to reconcile them. In part, by simply being one indivisible entity with an existence in the 'real world', yet displaying contradictory personality traits, stars can affirm that it is possible to triumph over, transcend, successfully live out contradictions. In the case of Turner, this centres on her being strongly sexual, both for herself and for others (therefore in Hollywood-American terms, extra-ordinary) but also ordinary. As Jeanine Basinger puts it, 'She was as much the ice cream parlor as she was the perfumed boudoir' (1976: 11). An interesting feature of Turner's career is that films and publicity seem continually to be condemning or punishing her for this daring combination, yet her survival and growth as an identification figure bespeak the hold of such a magic reconciliation of opposites on the cinematic imagination.

3 In Turner's later films, the processes of manufacture – the production of the image – are increasingly evident until they become an integral part of the image. With most stars, the point is to disguise the manufacturing so that they simply appear to be what their image proclaims them to be; with Turner, part of the fascination is with the manufacture itself – with her, it is actually beguiling to see the strings being pulled. This is especially true of *The Bad and the Beautiful* and *Imitation of Life*, and also of the Joe Morella and Edward Z. Epstein biography *Lana* (1972), which focuses as much on the fabrication of Lana as on the 'reality' of Judy Turner.

ZIEGFELD GIRL (1941)

Ziegfeld Girl inherits from Turner's previous career her sexy-ordinary image. In the process of building on it, however, the film gets severely out of joint, turning a production-values-laden musical into quite a serious drama. The Turner parts of the film make explicit what also comes across in the Judy Garland and Hedy Lamarr parts – a fumbling, confused critique of the notion of woman as spectacle at its most glorified, to wit, the Ziegfeld girl.

The sexy-ordinary configuration of the Turner image was crystallized in four moments in her career prior to *Ziegfeld Girl*: her first film role in *They Won't Forget* (1937), her sweater-girl pin-ups, her marriage to Artie Shaw and her starlet roles taken as a whole.

In *They Won't Forget*, she plays a young woman whose every action breathes sexuality – getting her male schoolteacher all flustered, telling a soda-jerk to put an egg in her malted milk 'as fresh as you', and walking down the street with hips swaying and breasts bouncing. She is raped and murdered. The ordinary setting and the ordinary clothes, together with the extraordinary appeal, would be enough to inflame any real man, the film seems to imply (and we never get to know who the rapist and murderer in fact is), and in so far as the film was a message film, it was a protest against the corruption of the South rather than against rape.

The sweater-girl pin-ups (Figure 8.1) date from Turner's appearance in *They Won't Forget*, but they became so widespread in the subsequent build-up that their meaning became rather more generalized. They encapsulate the sexy-ordinary configuration. On the one hand, a sweater is not a glamour garment – it is something cheap, practical, available everywhere. (In none of the portraits does Turner appear to be wearing an extravagantly styled sweater or one made of costly stuff.) On the other hand, worn by Turner, it became blatantly erotic, showing off the breasts, clinging to the waist. The rigid separation of women stars into homely-but-sexless (loose or flattening garments, including sweaters) or sexy-but-exotic (fetishistic fabrics, outlandish designs heightening body features) was collapsed. The girl-next-door was that never-never sex bombshell, plain-knit and voyeur's delight were one.

In February 1940, Turner eloped with Artie Shaw. Four months later, she divorced him. Although sex in a direct form was not mentioned in the coverage of these events, they are still an inflection of the sexy-ordinary configuration. Shaw was a band leader, and the bands were the courtship, dating, heterosexual romance music of the day. Turner's first marriage was at the heart of America's love-and-sex culture. It was also impulsive, although this was not necessarily viewed as a negative quality – it could be considered charmingly youthful, though it had already intimations of immaturity. More important, it was over in four months. Turner's publicly available life was going wrong; something was going sour in the heart of ordinariness.

Certain patterns of the Turner image, then, were beginning to take shape – sexiness perceived in ordinariness, but also associations of this with youth/immaturity and trouble. The starlet roles between *They Won't Forget* and *Ziegfeld Girl* do not appear to have elaborated upon this, but it is clear that the ambiguity of Turner's image was sufficient for MGM to feel equally happy casting her as a good girl (*We Who Are Young*, 1940) or a bad (*Love Finds Andy Hardy*, 1938), a sexpot (*Calling Dr Kildare*, 1939) or a down-to-earth student (*Dramatic School*, 1938). A star's physiognomy carries the meanings of her/his image in whatever film she or he makes, in whatever character she or he plays (cf. Alloway 1972). Thus, short of being strenuously performed against the image, it is likely that by 1940 the character played by Turner, just because it was played by her, was already sexy-ordinary, no matter whether the film made something of it or not and virtually regardless of the character as scripted.

Figure 8.1 The sweater girl

Ziegfeld Girl is very conscious of the images of its three main stars, Turner, Garland and Lamarr. Narrative and treatment are tailored to them. Garland is established as having a vaudeville background and thus all the know-how of the born-in-a-trunk pro; she is dressed in little-girl suits and has her requisite wistful follow-up to 'Over the Rainbow' in 'I'm Always Chasing Rainbows' as well as her jazzy, up-tempo spot, 'Minnie from Trinidad'. With Lamarr, everything promotes her remote, exotic beauty – she is foreign, married to a violinist (hence associated with Artistic Beauty), and has no thought of becoming a Ziegfeld girl when the star of the show (Frank Merton/Tony Martin) is stunned by her beauty as he passes her; a glistening close-up shot of her is often inserted into her scenes with other people (whereas it never is of Turner or Garland), which effectively sets her apart from the interaction; in the numbers, she is the statuesque central figure, coming closest to Ziegfeld's prescriptions for his 'girls'. The film's overall structure can accommodate these two images – they can be used effectively in the numbers, and fit two show-business women types (though, as I'll argue below, there are elements of criticism of Ziegfeld girlhood even in Lamarr and Garland). Turner (Sheila) fits less happily.

The film begins by building on the ordinary side of the Turner configuration. She is 'discovered' operating a lift in a department store. Neither a pro nor an exotic beauty, she is just an ordinary working girl rocketed to stardom. This conforms with the publicity surrounding Turner's own discovery at a soda fountain in a Hollywood Boulevard drug-store (this is inaccurate, though not drastically so), and meteoric rise to fame (it took rather longer than was publicly known). Her first act on being asked to audition for Ziegfeld is to go and try on an exorbitantly priced leopard-skin coat. This again conforms with her image as a girl who gets a real lift out of possessions. As one fan magazine of the period noted, 'She glitters whether on the beach, in the drawing room, or in the studio restaurant dressed in gingham. She admits she enjoys the luxury that stardom has brought her. And she drives a fire-engine red coupé. Lana is the most spectacular personality to be thrown up by films since Clara Bow.'

Thus far, *Ziegfeld Girl* is simply reproducing a facet of Turner's image. However, as both Basinger and Morella/Epstein state, during the making of the film, MGM and the director, Robert Z. Leonard, were so impressed by Turner that they expanded her role. This affects the film in three ways – building on the elements of the Turner image adds complexity to that image, the impact of her role comes into conflict with the musical's generic requirements, and her increasing centrality also calls into question the film's central motif.

Building on the image of the ordinary girl rocketed to a fame she luxuriates in brings in the complexity of response claimed by the Turner sexy-ordinary image. There is certainly a basic level of delight of the kind the fan magazine evinced. But there is also and equally pathos and condemnation. The impulsive desire to spend, and spend big, is perhaps in itself sympathetic, and is rendered more so in a key scene between Sheila/Turner and her old truck-driver boyfriend Gil (James Stewart). Her desire is located in deprivation, a deprivation the film is careful to link not with her class situation but with her unlucky experience as a child of always being the one who arrived at a party 'after the ice cream ran out'. We are asked to be sorry for her – doubly so when, running after Gil as he leaves in disgust, she trips on the minks she has strewn before him to proclaim her new wealth. We are here being asked to be sorry for her materialism, for what led to it in the first place and what it is doing to her now. Yet in her pursuit of wealth, she goes to the bad. She acquires a sugar daddy, Geoffrey, then, when he snubs her, she takes to drink, is suspended from the Follies and winds up in a seedy bar with Jimmy, also a down-and-out. It is no longer clear what sort of response is being elicited. She has broken taboos on women's behaviour – losing her man by demanding he adapt to her life-style, getting drunk. These demand condemnation by the conventions of the film's day, and I do not know how far the pathos elements let her off the hook. This ambiguity, the 'bad' woman who suffers for her badness and thus becomes an identification/ sympathy figure, is the emotional timbre that is caught in all her subsequent films.

As the dramatic-pathetic elements increase with Sheila/Turner's downfall, so they come to occupy the centre of the film. Not only does this mean that the other two star characters' careers are given short shrift (as narrative developments in musicals often are), but it also begins to interfere with what is a musical's *raison d'être*, the numbers. Throughout it is clear that the numbers do not quite know what to do with Turner – she has no musical gifts (or none that film has ever developed), and although she would be fine as one of the chorines in Busby Berkeley's Warners Depression musicals, the kind of thing Berkeley is staging here, all haughty parading and baroque head-dresses and trains, does not suit her small frame and 'common' face – not yet in her career, anyway. By the time of the last big production number, 'You Gotta Pull Strings', the Sheila/Turner plot dominates everything and, since the point is that she is not in this number, having been suspended from the Follies, the emotional weight in the cross-cutting between the number and her in the theatre watching is decidedly with her. All the more so when, unable to watch any more, despite having struggled out of her alcohol-induced sick-bed to be there, she leaves the auditorium and the film stays with her and not the number. As she hears the final walk-down music strike up on stage, she holds herself up and begins to walk down the entrance stairs. Thus for the climax of the number (and of all the numbers in the film) we see Turner in the 'surrounding' narrative and not the girls in the 'central' number.

This final walk-down also has a further significance in the film. The walk-down is the defining motif of the Ziegfeld show – it is the mo-ment at which the girls parade themselves and are thus 'glorified'. It is used five times in relation to Sheila/Turner. The first is in the first big production number, 'You Stepped out of a Dream' (Figure 8.2). In this, the camera follows Turner as she walks down the circling ramp. Garland and Lamarr are not similarly treated, although the latter is given a couple of cut-in close-ups of her sculptured face, and she is distinguished from both Garland and Turner by her dress, which is more *haute couture*, less show-girl in style. The effect of the camera sticking with Turner in this number, which for all three characters is their first night as Ziegfeld girls, is to stress her excitement at being a Ziegfeld girl and to associate the walk-down especially with her. The second use of the walk-down motif takes place the next morning at Turner's home (she is still living with her parents): she is trudging down the stairs until her brother says, 'Here comes the glamour girl!' – then she straightens up, and descends the stairs as if on stage for the walk-down (Figure 8.3). Again, in the night-club in Florida, she walks down some stairs as if she and they are in the Follies, only this time it is after quarrelling with Gil and drinking too much champagne. Each walk-down is registering a moment in her career. The next is on stage, in the 'Minnie from Trinidad' number, during which she collapses, drunk, and the last is during 'You Gotta Pull Strings', as described above.

The walk-down motif in relation to Sheila/Turner links her decline – which the film, as we've seen, also explains in terms of deprivation, materialism and going to the bad – to the core of the Zeigfeld show. In this way, by association, the whole enterprise of Ziegfeld – his girls, woman as spectacle – which the film was clearly set up to celebrate, is called into question. There are intimations of this through the Garland and Lamarr characters. The only one of the three to make it to the top is Garland – but then she has her roots in vaudeville, which is signalled in the film, through the character of her father, as being a more vital and authentic entertainment tradition. (Her father is played by Charles Winniger; in the film he teams up with Al Shean in a re-creation of Gallagher and Shean, one of the legendary acts on the vaudeville circuit; this happens just before the enfeebled 'You Gotta Pull Strings' number and 'brings the house down'; effectively, vaudeville has the last say in the film's numbers.) Lamarr, on the other hand, leaves the Follies to join her husband when he gets a job; the very haughty beauty which makes her an epitome of the Ziegfeld girl also makes her 'superior' to show business. Between Garland and Lamarr, Ziegfeld gets it from low and high-brows.

What Sheila/Turner adds to this is sex. Clearly, despite the 'Glorifying the American girl' tag, Ziegfeld was peddling sexuality – but the glorification idea, his use of famous couturiers and chic designers, appeared to elevate his shows above the despised burlesque (which means striptease in American usage). Sheila/Turner drags it down again. Partly, the film takes on Turner's association with sexuality just by having her in it. In addition, some of the dialogue draws attention to the Ziegfeld project, as when Patsy (Eve Arden) wisecracks to the girls about their make-up, 'Don't worry dear, they won't be looking at your face.' It is on Sheila/Turner's legs that the camera dwells in this first walk-down, aided by the wide parting in her sequined dress. And, again unlike Garland or Lamarr, it is as a pin-up that she acquires off-stage fame, even winding up on the wall of the garage where Gil works. The crystallization of all this round Sheila/Turner and her special association with the walk-down motif puts a dent in the hypocrisy of Ziegfeld's glittering sex show. Add to that the emotional weighting given her, her virtually eclipsing the numbers by the end, and one can see how the decision to build on Turner's star image leads the film almost to overturn its own project. The brief scene of reconciliation with Gil (they are going to go to the

Figure 8.2 The end of a walk-down: 'You Stepped out of a Dream' from *Ziegfeld Girl*

Figure 8.3 The end of a walk-down at home in *Ziegfeld Girl*

country to breed ducks) and a perfunctory shot of Garland atop a wedding-cake-style set hardly suffice to set the film properly back on course.

THE POSTMAN ALWAYS RINGS TWICE (1946)

Between *Ziegfeld Girl* and *Postman*, Turner's sexy-ordinary image was consolidated. The war proved useful for this. Nothing is more ordinary in the public imagination than the serviceman. Thus the fact that, for instance, the sailors of the SS *Idaho* voted her their favourite star, that she married a serviceman in life (Stephen Crane) and in a film (*Marriage is a Private Affair*, 1944), and herself joined the WACS in *Keep Your Powder Dry* (1945), all preserved her association with ordinariness. Equally, they preserved the association of that with other things – with plain sexiness in the case of the SS *Idaho* men – and throughout the war Turner was a major pin-up in men's magazines. The marriage to Crane (1942) went wrong – she married on impulse again, as with Shaw, knowing next to nothing about him; he was, however, already married, so the marriage had to be annulled; then he got a divorce, but she would not remarry him and he tried to commit suicide twice; she discovered she was pregnant and they remarried; a year later (1944) they divorced, with Turner getting custody of the baby, Cheryl. Following the Shaw fiasco, it was as if Turner and marriage (ordinary marriage to ordinary men) did not go. Not that Shaw or Crane came out of it well, but both marriages set off the central Turner ambiguity – what she touches turns bad, but is that because she is bad or because she is irresistibly attracted to the bad? (And is being attracted to the bad itself badness?) *Marriage is a Private Affair* similarly dealt with a GI's marriage (after a three-day courtship) going off the rails, through his wife's (Turner's) infidelity, though all ends happily. More generally, Turner's status as sexy leading lady was confirmed by her teamings with Clark Gable in *Honky Tonk* (1941) and *Somewhere I'll Find You* (1942).

These ambiguities, the role of impulse, the play on badness and on the sexy-ordinary configuration, all came in useful for the Turner character, Cora, in *Postman*. Without them, the film courts incoherence in its construction of this central character.

I want to consider *Postman* chiefly in terms of the key but neglected question of how a character is constructed in a film. What I want to suggest is that there are here three different methods of character construction, which fit uneasily together. These methods are structural (we understand characters by what they do in the plot or how they function in the narrative), motivational (the reasons provided by dialogue and sometimes other elements such as performance and *mise-en-scène* as to why a character does such-and-such a thing) and star-based (the star's image already gives the character a certain set of traits). These methods contribute to the construction of an apparently autonomous character (rather than one acknowledged as an aspect of the film's point(s)-of-view) – corresponding, of course, to how we normally talk about characters, ascribing motives and feelings to them as if they are real people independent of us and a narrative's author.

The initial problem with *Postman* is who the film is really about. Structurally, it is a *film noir*, which means that, like nearly all *films noirs*, the narrative is centred on the male protagonist (Frank/John Garfield). His voice-over leads into the film and recurs at various points until we realize he has been telling his story to a priest in prison. Since the film ends there and a priest has been the listener, a certain status is conferred retrospectively on Frank as both the subject of the narrative and its truthful narrator. The film can then be seen as being 'about' the hero's doom. The sense of doom, fate, entrapment is reinforced by the obsessive doubling of events and images in the film, both major narrative incidents (two accidents with a lorry, two attempts to kill the husband Nick, two attempts to leave the café, two trials for murder) and minor details of treatment (two lipstick rolls, two vital notes left in the cash register, two pushes at the car on the second attempt on Nick's life, the echoes at the lake, the name of the café, The Twin Oaks, and the title of the film).

In this context, the woman is a function of the ensnaring structure. The *femme fatale* need not necessarily be evil, but she is the means by which the hero gets drawn into the plot, and hence his doom. Indeed, it is more to the point if she is not simply and utterly evil, for it is precisely the hero's uncertainty on this point, the very unknowability of Woman, that really traps him. (Much of the pleasure of *film noir* resides in the true knowledge of the woman, as good or evil, vouchsafed the hero and hence the (male?) audience at the end; e.g. *The Maltese Falcon*, *The Lady from Shanghai*, *Chinatown*.)

At one level, Cora in *Postman* is a mere function of the film's structure. She is only there to be the means by which Frank enters the path that leads to his doom, to be the terrible object of his sexuality, terrible because his attraction to her is what leads him to the death cell. Her famous first appearance – the roll of her lipstick along the floor attracting his (and the camera's) attention, followed by a track back along the floor, up her bare legs to her white shorts and halter top – is very directly sexual, and throughout the film her brilliant white clothes are both eye-catching and a sign of the heat of the summer (with all that connotes). The wretchedness of women, in the mind of *film noir*, is that they are such a turn-on for the hero, with disastrous consequences for him (compare the logic of *They Won't Forget*). One can see Cora functioning like this throughout the film's structure.

Yet even in the first scene, it is not as simple as that. On the one hand,

Cora as herself a subject is implied – the 'Man Wanted' sign in the opening shots of the film hangs over the scene, we can assume she has rolled the lipstick herself, and the manner in which she does her lips while looking at him suggests a deliberate making of herself into an object of desire. On the other hand, the burning hamburger, so obviously a symbol of lighted passions, and the general atmosphere of heat suggest a sexual force generated between them both (a sense referred to by almost every reviewer as 'the chemistry' 'sparked' between Garfield and Turner). A sense of Cora as herself a force acting on the narrative derives from the motivational level of character construction in *Postman* being as emphatic as the structural. Cora, and Cora-and-Frank, are provided with reasons for doing things, whereas in other *films noirs* only Frank would be.

Yet as soon as this motivational level comes into play, further problems arise. If one looks at the motives Cora is provided with, they are ambiguous and contradictory almost to the point of incoherence. Why, as indicated by the film, does Cora get Frank to kill Nick? Because, pitiably, she is trapped into a marriage with a dreary older man, largely because she was fed up with other men bothering her ('I was never homey . . . I never met a man since I was fifteen who didn't want to give me an argument about it'). And because she is ambitious (her repeated statements to the effect that she wants 'to make something' of herself and the café). And because she loves Frank (she leaves the café with him; her direct, i.e. 'genuine', outburst in the kitchen after she has been contemplating suicide with a kitchen knife, 'If you really love me, you would . . .'), and/or is manipulating him (in an earlier kitchen scene, we get a close-up on 'Can't you see how happy we'd be together?' in which her shifting eyes clearly signal manipulation). And because she is driven by a bad sexuality (the scenes on the beach; her provocative clothes; images of heat). Partly, what is happening here is that the film wants to give Cora motivations, including some that make her a sympathetic figure, but, as her (generic) function in the narrative is to be changeable and unknowable, the film has to keep giving her different, inconsistent motivations. Yet inconsistency on this scale risks being simply incoherent. The film's devices would betray themselves all too quickly without Lana Turner in the part.

Because it is Turner, the contradictions of Cora, and Cora-and-Frank, get an emphasis which amounts to a resolution (more or less – perceptions will differ on this). Cora is sexy-ordinary: her speech about not being 'homey' indicates this clearly enough, as indeed does the extraordinary sexual charge she carries in so suffocatingly dull a setting. The various motivations she is provided with can be loosely organized around the badness syndrome developed in Turner's image. She is attracted to the bad (adultery, murder); this makes her pitiable (she is trapped both by her situation of marriage and by the inexorable repetitions of the plot once she strays from marriage), but it also intimates that she may herself be bad (her sexuality, her manipulation and prompting of Frank to murder). Notions of coherence of character do not permit the coexistence of such traits (except under the rubric of woman the capricious and unknowable, which is not allowable here since, on the contrary, we know too much, and of that much is sympathetic), but notions of the star reconciling or holding in tension key contradictions in the culture (and thus effectively transcending them) do permit them to a certain extent. However, in the process, certain traits are subordinated. Thus Cora's driving ambition, which is granted legitimacy at the motivational level simply in terms of the time allowed it and the straight treatment of it, lacks force since it has no place in the Turner complex. As a result, one either ignores the ambition motive, or denies it legitimacy by regarding it as falsehood or manipulation, or merely feels that it does not fit.

The motivations of Cora-and-Frank, as a couple and as murderers, are also aided by Turner's presence, though here she is less crucial to the film's coherence. The key to their murderous relationship is impulse. In each of the scenes in which they contemplate murder, a crash of music, where before there was none, signals the thought of murder arising from nowhere rational in their minds. The first of these scenes occurs after Nick, returning drunk from the laundry, nearly crashes into a lorry. Frank blurts out, 'I'd like to see him get plastered like that and drive off a cliff'; music in; they look at each other as Cora says, 'You didn't mean that, you were joking', and Frank replies, ''Course I was'; they kiss. The idea for murder arises spontaneously; music signals its impact; a kiss links it to passion. (In an earlier scene, Frank's suggestion of Cora wanting to make money so as to have some set aside when her husband dies is also met by music and a kiss, though murder as such is not mentioned.) The second such scene takes place in Frank's bedroom. Having elicited from him that he loves her, Cora, fingering the lapel of the dressing-gown he is wearing, says, 'There's one thing we could do.' Frank replies, 'Pray for something to happen to Nick,' and Cora says, 'Something like that'; music in; Frank exclaims, 'Cora!' Here the link between passion and murder is clearer, but murder is not actually directly referred to. It is clearly in Cora's mind, but she does not have to say the word for Frank to latch on. The music signals its arousal in their 'chemistry'. The third scene takes place in the kitchen, after Frank has discovered Cora with a kitchen knife in her hand. Here there is a more directly expressed impulsive outburst from Cora – 'If you really love me, you would . . .'; pause; Frank, 'All right'; music in; Cora, 'No!' This last exclamation suggests that the idea for murder arose in her head without premeditation. Once again, the music suggests the intention to murder is an impulse rather than a rational or cold-blooded plan.

The film, then, does a lot of work on the notion of impulse, even without the input of Turner as Cora. The particular inflection she adds is suffering from one's own impulses. Her impulsive marriages in life had led to suffering of one kind and another, and the film roles reprised this. Consequently the pattern of impulse and entrapment in *Postman* can be read – I would argue, *was* read by Turner's fans – as a source of identification and sympathy. The attraction to bad (often meaning little more than sexual desire) can be seen as an uncontrollable, destroying impulse that anyone can identify with (especially in a sex-negative culture). Yet this means that, at the level of the star image's contribution to character, the film is about Cora at least as much as it is about Frank, even though structurally she is a mere function of his destiny. Thus, if in terms of the relationship between the motivational and star image levels, Turner serves to mask the contradictions of the *femme fatale* type (a type of course that reflects the male construction – and fear – of the female), in terms of the relationship between the structural and star levels, Turner serves to open up the tension between what women are for men and what that means for women as women. (I am not positing here either any brilliance on Turner's part – though I would never wish to denigrate her performing abilities – nor an untutored feminist sensibility on the part of director, writer, or whoever; it is rather that in the relationship between her life/films and women audiences, a certain registering and defining of the female experience in this society was possible and that this happens in *Postman* simply because she is in it.) If that accounts for the film's near-incoherence and unsatisfactory feel, it also accounts for the fascination of its elusive play of fate and motivation.

THE BAD AND THE BEAUTIFUL (1953)

In both *Ziegfeld Girl* and *Postman*, Turner's image contributes to the overall meaning of the film, partially undermining it in the former, largely coming to its rescue in the latter. With *The Bad and the Beautiful* (1953) and *Imitation of life* (1959), the image becomes itself in part the subject-matter of the film. By this time, however, the image's meaning has shifted in certain respects. The sexy-ordinary configuration has become 'glamour' (or, 'Lanallure'), and the badness both more extreme and more pitiable. Both these developments are reproduced, and celebrated, in *The Bad and the Beautiful*.

Glamour and ordinariness are antithetical notions. The ordinary and the everyday are by definition not glamorous. Yet glamour – or the particular inflection of the notion embodied by Turner – is based on manufacture, and can be seen to be the process, the industrial process, by which the ordinary is rendered the glamorous. The glamour industry, in which Hollywood played a decisive part, sold itself on the idea that, given its products, anyone – any woman, anyway – could become beautiful. Turner was living proof of this, and if, later in her career, none of the original material – the ordinary woman – showed through any more, this was all the more proof that the glamour process worked.

Turner's career as a pin-up illustrates this transition and also helps to identify the notion of glamour. The early examples make reference to the social world as a whole, outside of Hollywood. In Figure 8.4, taken when she was 17 (1938), this is done by a certain 'naturalism'. Artful as the photo actually is, it is meant to look spontaneous, just catching the girl on a turn, and we are not supposed to notice the elements of lighting, retouching, etc. The loosely coiffed hair, the type of expression, the apparent absence of make-up, all impose a notion of a natural, ordinary girl. Figure 8.5, on the other hand, is very obviously a studio photograph (taken in 1940) with its 'odd' angle, arch pose and obvious set. Yet despite that', it is still full of social referents – the 'bad girl' expression, the tousled (= sexually loose) hair, the dress with its busy jungle print. The social reference of the sweater-girl pin-ups has already been discussed. Thus, for all their artifice, whether or not obvious, these photographs do relate Turner to social types, attitudes, values and life-styles in the 'everyday world'. (The everyday world is of course a fiction – it is not the world that we actually experience every day, but rather the world that we assume is *typically* experienced by other people. Needless to add, much of the definition of what constitutes the typically everyday derives from the mass media.) The later examples, on the other hand, refer to a self-enclosed, self-defined world of glamour. The images are static, the compositional values less dynamic (compare the half-turn of the head and holding of the pearls in Figure 8.6 with the sharp round-over-the-shoulder look of Figures 8.4 and 8.5, or compare the essentially circular pattern made by the later examples, the arms serving to bring the eye back to the body, with the sweater-girl pose of Figure 8.1 – the arms thrust away from the body and the thrusting breasts and knees). These later pin-ups (they date from 1958–60) inhabit a glazed, plastic, perfectly 'finished' world. Any movement would disturb the lighting, as it catches the hair in Figure 8.6, moulds the face in Figure 8.7 and creates patterns in Figure 8.8. And the only reference outside this world is to the world of glamorous consumption – expensive possessions such as pearls, furs, evening dresses and expensive services of hairdressing and cosmetics. This self-enclosed world of glamour, glorying in its own artifice, is brought into sharper focus by the press photograph (taken in 1951) of Turner with her friend Ava Gardner (Figure 8.9). Gardner represents a notion of natural, 'animal' beauty. Although this is as manufactured as any other image of beauty, the manufacture is less obvious – her hair is loosely dressed, she wears a plain blouse and

simple pearls, her expression is direct. Turner on the other hand bes-
peaks manufacture in every detail, down to the slightly held-off pose
against Gardner.

It is this element of manufactured glamour that is emphasized in
The Bad and the Beautiful. Whenever there is a break in the filming
within the film, a hairdresser or make-up artist steps in to retouch
Georgia/Turner's look (they are in fact played by Turner's personal
hairdresser, Helen Young, and make-up man, Del Armstrong). The
screen-test sequence opens with a close-up of her eyebrow being
painted in – as any assiduous reader of the fan magazines would have
known, Turner had had her eyebrows shaved off for the role of an
oriental handmaiden during the filming of *The Adventures of Marco Polo*
in 1938, and they never grew again. This shot is (like the casting of
hairdresser and make-up man) part in-joke, but also part reinforce-
ment of the idea of the manufacture of glamour, not just by heightening beauty that is already there but also by creating artificial beauty
where there is nothing.

By emphasizing manufacture, the film also emphasizes the star image as an illusion. This is evoked in the first shot of Georgia/Turner. A
maid answers the phone and says it is Mr Shields; the camera moves
across (is it to another room, or was the maid a reflection in a mirror?),
showing us in quick succession first Georgia side-on in a mirror, then
her back, then her face full-on in a mirror. Already the film is giddy
with reflection images, reflections, moreover, of a woman preparing
her appearance at a dressing-table. How can we, as we watch, pick out
the levels of illusion here? – the illusion of reflection, the illusion of
make-up, the illusion of the film we are watching . . . Georgia/Turner
puts a black lace veil over her head, then turns to listen at the tele-
phone receiver. The camera now finally homes in on her face (rather
than the reflection of it), stopping at a perfectly composed glamour
framing. The final frame of this brief one-take, then, is both really
Georgia (or Turner . . .), not her reflection, and yet is also she at her
most 'produced'.

What we have got in the final frame is the *real illusion*. For it is no part
of the purpose of *The Bad and the Beautiful* to demystify glamour by
foregrounding its manufacture. Rather, the processes of manufacture
themselves become fascinating and . . . glamorous. The same holds true
for the film's overall depiction of Hollywood. It is rather like a conjuror
showing you how a trick is done by quickness of the hand – you are so
impressed by the dexterity that you remain as dazzled by how the trick
is done as you were before by its magic effect. (This relates to Minnelli's
other films; cf. Cook 1977.)

Nor is this emphasis on the glamour of illusion-manufacture meant to
detract from the notion of the star's special quality or magic. On the
contrary, it is the techniques of illusion that stimulate the 'real magic' of

Figure 8.4 Early pin-up of Lana Turner I

Figure 8.5 Early pin-up of Lana Turner II

Figure 8.6 Later pin-up of Lana Turner I

Figure 8.7 Later pin-up of Lana Turner II

Figure 8.8 Later pin-up of Lana Turner III

Figure 8.9 Lana Turner and Ava Gardner in greeting

the star, the 'truth' of her 'performance'. (The oxymoronic brilliance of *The Bad and the Beautiful* will finally defeat me.) In the dialogue, we have repeated insistences that Georgia is a star. This has nothing to do with talent or acting ability but, as Jonathan (Kirk Douglas) says after her screen-test, the fact that, no matter how bad she may be, no one can take their eyes off her when she is on the screen. Similarly, Jonathan dismisses Lucien's objection that Georgia does not have the poise for a period costume the former has designed, observing that Georgia is a star and will therefore be all right. She needs only to be tutored to bring out this innate quality. In the processing of the raw material, the hidden value – star quality – will be revealed. (The film apparently wants to insist that this is not a question of conning the public – nowhere in *The Bad and the Beautiful* is the apparatus of fan magazines, promotion and so on shown directly to have a role in star manufacture, although the press agent, Syd, is seen as a permanent member of the creative studio team.)

In the working-out of the narrative, this play on reality and illusion comes to a mesmerizing climax. Jonathan cannot get the right effect from Georgia in the marriage scene in the film they are shooting. When they pack up for the day, they have a quiet exchange during which Georgia gazes longingly at him. 'That's the expression I want!' he says. As a result, Georgia pours her feeling for him into the role in the film. It is this that gives 'truth' to her performance. Yet the film has hinted, and is soon to reveal, that he is merely manipulating her. In other words, the truth of her performance rests on a deception.

When Georgia herself realizes this, discovering him at home with another woman during the première party, we have the famous car scene, in which, in one long take, she drives into the night, crying hysterically, with headlights glaring into her (and our) eyes, the rain lashing down, the camera twisting around her. What we seem to be getting here is the moment of real reality, assured by the notion that only untrammelled, chaotic, violent emotion is authentic. All the rest is illusion. It is the supreme masterstroke to fabricate this authenticity so completely in a studio mock-up of a car and with the epitome of star artifice, Lana Turner.

Turner's association with badness continued as a defining element of her publicly available private life between *Postman* and *The Bad and the Beautiful*. She dated countless men, most of them famous, and hence was widely rumoured to be a nymphomaniac (or, as an MGM executive quoted by Morella and Epstein revealingly put it, 'Lana had the morals and the attitudes of a man. . . . If she saw a muscular stage hand with tight pants and she liked him, she'd invite him into her dressing-room'). In 1947, she married Bob Topping, a wealthy heir, three days after his divorce from a previous marriage (in which she was named as co-respondent). The Presbyterian minister who married them was, with much publicity directed against Turner, suspended because Presbyterians are not allowed to marry people divorced for less than a year. In 1951, she was separated from Topping; she had an accident in her shower, variously put down to drunkenness, suicide attempt, or pure accident. The films of the period, however – apart from her role as the thoroughly wicked Lady de Winter in *The Three Musketeers* (1948) – do not reflect this emphasis on badness. What does characterize them, apart from their use of Turner as a glamour object, is a tendency to team her with considerably older men, including Spencer Tracy in *Cass Timberlaine* (1947) and a visibly ageing Clark Gable in *Homecoming* (1948; this was their third film together, but the difference in their ages was more apparent than before).

This teaming is of a piece with the emergence in Turner's publicity, as crucially related to her association with badness, of the role of her father. Early in her career, MGM had invented a biography for Turner, giving her a wealthy father ('a mining engineer') who had died in an accident. In fact, she came from a very poor home; her father, who had once been a miner, was a gambler and bootlegger and was murdered by one of his cronies when Turner was ten. The studio had wanted to fabricate Turner as an All American Girl – but when her image was clearly anything but harmed by her turning to the bad, it became useful to let the true story of Turner's past be known via fan magazines, biographies, etc. The inexorable link with badness, and its pitiability, was strengthened by the image of both her sordid origins and her loss of her father. This got her all ways: she was indelibly bad, but could not help it, genetically (who her father was), environmentally (the upbringing he gave her) and psychologically (loss of him at a crucial age made the passage to mature heterosexuality problematic). In a culture as drenched, even at the popular level, in naturalizing, individuated explanations of personality as America in the 1940s and 1950s, Turner and her father were a powerful image-complex. In an interview, Turner herself suggested the meaning of her father's death – 'Since my life has been wayward and impulsive, always a search for something that is not there, and then disillusionment, I believe I need all the excuses I can make. The shock I suffered then may be a valid excuse for me now. It may explain things I do not myself understand' (quoted by Morella and Epstein).

The idea that Turner's relations with men are somehow related to the early death of her father gives a certain *frisson* to many of her roles – for example, Sheila has a sugar daddy in *Ziegfeld Girl*, Nick in *Postman* is old enough to be Cora's father. But this is all very oblique. With *The Bad and the Beautiful*, it is the key to the relationship between Georgia and Jonathan. What follows is not a psychoanalytic reading of *The Bad and the Beautiful*, much less of Georgia and Jonathan; it is rather an analysis of a text that is, rather obviously, informed by popular psychoanalysis, as indeed many films directed by Vincente Minnelli are. Their fathers bring them together; her dependence upon him depends upon her rejecting her real father and replacing him with Jonathan; the question is whether she can in turn reject this surrogate father.

Their fathers bring them together, although both are dead. Georgia's father, an actor, worked for Jonathan's, a producer, just as Georgia and Jonathan are actor and producer respectively. Georgia's father drew a picture of Jonathan's father, as a demon with a pitchfork, on the (?nursery) wall of his home. It is here that Jonathan and Georgia (legs only visible, dangling from a loft) first meet. Jonathan removes the drawing from the wall, and hangs it in his office. When she goes, an unknown bit player, for an audition there, it is her turning to look at the drawing (together with her lustrous blonde hair seen earlier when she is working as a stand-in) that identifies her to Jonathan. It is moreover her turning, with an identical movement of the head, to look at the drawing in studio boss Harry Pebbel's office in the film's framing story that leads into her flashback of her relationship with Jonathan. This relationship is thus signalled at various important moments by her father's hostile feelings towards his father.

He 'kills' her father. She has 'built a shrine to him' (Jonathan's words) and he breaks it up, smashing the record of her father intoning a *Macbeth* soliloquy, drawing a moustache on a picture of him. As a result, she is free of her father – but by substituting Jonathan. In the scene after he has dropped her in the pool (she has gone out and got drunk through fear on the night before shooting begins), Georgia/Turner performs just like a little girl. The accoutrements of glamour are replaced by a head towel and outsize coat (it is his, but it makes her look like the archetypal little girl wearing a grown-up's clothes). She sits first on the floor, then on his knee – never in an equal adult position. She speaks, in a little-girl voice, such cute lines as, 'If we were married, I wouldn't take up much room.' And he tells her, 'Love is for the very young.' The naughty little girl, legs dangling out of the loft in the scene of their first meeting, has become the good, meek daughter. She has become his child.

The elision of the sexual and parental in this development is precisely the point – it is the sexuality of daughter–father relationships, and the dangerous sexual consequences of their disruption, that are played on in the Turner image and in the Georgia–Jonathan relationship. In turn, this relates to the theme of her becoming 'authentic'. Just as the car scene signals an explosion of 'real' feeling, so, too, with rather fewer stops pulled out, does the climax of the scene in her bedroom, where Jonathan smashes her father's 'shrine'. He has sneered at her – 'Look at you, you're acting now, playing the doomed daughter of the great man' – and when he smashes the shrine, she attacks him, her hair comes loose and swings in the light. In both cases, the 'real' feeling is signalled by a departure from the static, perfectly groomed look of Georgia/Turner to wild movement with textures (her hair here, her fur in the car scene) that capture and diffuse the light. And in both cases she is being required, forcibly, to reject her father (real or surrogate).

Whether she does succeed, however, in freeing herself from her second father, Jonathan – and hence, like the Turner image, from a father-fixated sexuality – is ambiguous. At the beginning of the film, just before she, together with Fred and James Lee, goes into Pebbel's office, she draws a moustache on the shield outside, Jonathan's emblem, exactly the same as the moustache he, Jonathan, draws on her father's portrait (later in the film, though earlier in her 'life'). She laughs with the others. This is clearly an act of defiance, doing to Jonathan what he did to her father. But perhaps it has to be read as only an act, not a real rejection. This is what the film suggests elsewhere. In the framing narrative she is dressed in black (a neat, tight-fitting suit), her hair drawn back. In the flashbacks, she wears light, usually white, clothes, and her hair hangs lustrously. The general contrast, and especially the cut back from the flashing car scene to her immobile, black figure, posed in recall, suggest repression. She is keeping unwanted desire in check, which is not the same thing as being free from it. She tells James Lee that one may grow out of first love, 'but you never get over it'. Directly, this means Jonathan, but, given the pattern of father references in the film, it could also mean her father – or fathers in general. Georgia has grown out of that (the 'mature' repression of desire in adulthood) but not got over it (still hung up on father figures). Of Turner, only the latter was touted as being the case. In the last shot of the film, she, like Fred and James Lee, remains fascinated by Jonathan, unable just to walk out, compelled to pick up the phone to hear what his ideas are. He still exercises his hold on her.

Whether this hold is a father–son one in the case of Fred and James Lee, I'm not sure. What does seeem a reasonable supposition is that Jonathan himself is free of his own father. Despite keeping up appearances (paying mourners to attend his father's funeral), he befriends the only man, Fred, who speaks against his father, pronounces his father '*the* heel' and seems to accept Georgia's father's view of him as a demon. He overthrows Pebbel, who is effectively in the position of his father, as head of the studio, and treats him with all the patronizing air of the still vigorous son. Jonathan is free of his father, but Georgia really is not. Perhaps this is because psychoanalytic thought only allows sons to kill fathers. Thus Georgia, like Turner, must remain pitiably locked into her perverse needs and desires.

IMITATION OF LIFE (1959)

By the time of *Imitation of Life* in 1959, the glamour emphasis in Turner's image had become uppermost. As Jeanine Basinger puts it, 'Turner appeared to cut loose her past. For the audience, it ceased to exist. She was their movie goddess – born and raised on film for their pleasure – the product of photogenesis' (1976: 17). The 'bad' elements continued before and after *Imitation of Life*, if anything more scandalous – four more marriages and divorces (Lex Barker 1953–7, Fred May 1960–2, Robert Eaton 1965–9, Ronald Dante 1969), accused of breaking up the marriage of Ava Gardner and Frank Sinatra, her daughter's involvement in various scandals (drugs, becoming a stripper, not to mention the Johnny Stompanato affair discussed below), and some film roles: *The Prodigal* (1955) as a wicked priestess, *Portrait in Black* (1960) as an adulterous murderer. However, the effect of all these was more to increase her glamorous otherness and to make her an identification figure, the suffering woman of the woman's film genre. It is these qualities that *Imitation of Life* capitalizes upon. More precisely, it uses a quality of 'detachment' characterizing Turner's dress and acting styles.

Throughout the films and public appearances of the 1950s, and on into the 1960s, Turner became increasingly associated with clothes. The 1965 film *Love Has Many Faces* was sold principally on the strength of its 'million dollar wardrobe', and the connection between Turner and a certain kind of dress-style was essential to the films she made for Ross Hunter (*Imitation of Life, Portrait in Black, Madame X* (1966)). Although many different designers worked on her films, notably Edith Head (*Who's got the Action?* (1962), *Love Has Many Faces*), Jean Louis (*Imitation of Life, Portrait in Black, Madame X*), Helen Rose (*A Life of Her Own* (1950), *The Merry Widow* (1952), *The Bad and the Beautiful, Latin Lovers* (1953), *Bachelor in Paradise* (1961)) and Travilla (*The Rains of Ranchipur* (1955), *The Big Cube* (1969)), and although the style very clearly belongs to American 1950s *haute couture*, there is none the less a certain Lana Turner look. This is prominent in *Imitation of Life* and relates to the film's elaboration of what is implied by its title.

The signification of many of the features of the look are those of *haute couture* in general, notably expensiveness (especially, with Turner, jewellery, elaborate head-dresses and hair-dos) and, distinguishing the wearer from those whose clothes have to permit labour, inconvenience (for Turner, trains, elaborate folds in the skirt, off-the-shoulder dresses). Certain other features are more specifically Lana: the use of man-made fibres, so that her high style is associated with glossy, modern artifice rather than 'natural' or 'old-fashioned' values; a quality of hardness in the clear-cut edges of the designs and in the use of colour, which, together with a tendency towards designs that create geometrical patterns around her frame, 'dehumanizes' her, plays down qualities of softness, roundness, even warmth; and a certain type of creation that is frankly bizarre and unimaginable outside of movies, even of Turner, such as an outfit in *Imitation of Life* consisting of vermilion pants and top, pink necklace, and a piece of pink flower-printed, insubstantial material shaped like an open-fronted dress, cut away at the knees, and trailing out behind in a full spread (Figure 8.10). The emphasis, then, is on artifice (a feature of the Turner image already dwelt upon), femininity (but one conceived not in terms of softness, but in terms of elaborateness, ornamentation, plasticity) and sheer impracticality, without connection with ordinary life. The net effect in many of her films is that Turner, in her fabulous costumes, is visually detached from her surroundings – India in *The Rains of Ranchipur*, Cornwall in *Another Time Another Place* (1958), a rusty old steamship, captained by John Wayne, in *The Sea Chase* (1955) – except in those cases where the set-up is itself equally 'unreal': as high priestess of Astarte in *The Prodigal* (revealing clothes that make every movement hazardous), as the richest woman in the world in *Latin Lovers* (in Brazil), and in *Love Has Many Faces* (in Acapulco). In *A Life of Her Own* and *Peyton Place* (1957) she was associated directly with *haute couture* as, respectively, a top model and owner of the town's smartest fashion salon.

The sense that all this gives to many of her film appearances – of her being detached from the events, on show – is central in *Imitation of Life*, for in it she plays a character, Lora, who is, or becomes, a person on show, performing, presenting an image, to be thought of neither as an essence (i.e. an inner human being expressing her self through presentation) nor as interacting with others and circumstances. In the early scenes in the film, she wears ordinary, everyday clothes – blouses and skirts, a suit for interview – but as she gradually becomes an actor and a star, her wardrobe becomes more and more Lana. If 'life' is essence, interaction, vitality, reality, then Lora/Turner, in her outlandish outfits, is an imitation of it. The problem the film poses (thus bringing in the suffering element in the Turner image) is whether there is, in fact, anything but imitation in life.

The key metaphor for imitation in the film is that of acting. The fact that Lora is an actor, in the professional sense, is only part of this. We never see her on stage, except in rehearsal or taking a bow. In so far as her profession is relevant to the metaphor of acting, it is in the way that she is set up as 'an actress' quite apart from any ability to act well on a stage. Thus agent Allen Loomis takes her on because he is impressed by her impersonation of an archetypal Hollywood star (this is how she inveigles her way into his office) and he wants to promote her not by putting her into a play but by taking her to parties *dressed like* an actress (in particular, in mink). Ironically, the only time we get to know anything about a play she is in is when she takes a part as a social worker in

Figure 8.10 Lanallure in *Imitation of Life*

a bid for realism. But Lora/Turner acts, puts on a performance, throughout the film. Detached by dress, she is further detached by acting style. Turner has a habit – in her other later films as well – of turning away from the person she is acting with to deliver a line, adopting a posture, head-on to camera although not actually looking into the camera. Even when she does not do this, her acting none the less is poised and posed. If one takes as an example someone at the very opposite end of the scale to her, Judy Garland, one can observe how Garland hangs on her acting partner's every word, watching her/his lips or eyes, registering response in minute facial inflections. It is this that gives Garland's performances their characteristically nervy, tense and spontaneous feel. By contrast, Turner's beautifully made-up face moves very little and she does not even always look at her partner. All of this is emphasized time and again in *Imitation of Life*, until the climactic moment when, turning from her sobbing daughter Susie (Sandra Dee), she declares, staring ahead of her, that she will give up Steve (John Gavin) rather than have him come between them. Susie looks at her and says, 'Oh mother, stop acting!' The film here draws attention to Turner's posing acting style, making its use of the style to embody 'imitation' explicit.

This use of Turner was given a further emotional charge for contemporary viewers by Turner's involvement in the trial of her daughter Cheryl for the murder of her (Turner's) boyfriend Johnny Stompanato (in 1958). More than one newspaper described her testimony as 'the greatest performance of her life.' Whether or not this was fair of the press, the confusion was compounded by the purely coincidental release of *Peyton Place* around the time of the trial. In it, Turner's big scene has her breaking down in sobs on the witness stand, just as she did at the Stompanato trial. There are of course further overtones of the Stompanato affair in the relationship between Steve and Susie (just as rumour had it that Cheryl had fallen for Johnny), again blurring the distinction between imitation and reality, screen and life.

Acting is only one of the many images for imitation of life used by the film. All of these (for instance, a Nat King Cole substitute to sing the title song; the use of an obviously artificial, stage-set-like backdrop for Lora's home; narrative touches such as having a job writing envelopes to give them a wholly spurious 'personal touch') connect to the central metaphor of acting/performance, but unlike *The Bad and the Beautiful*, with its endless reflections and cross-references which trap everything in the paradoxes of illusionism, *Imitation of Life* does also point, in an ultimately very melancholic fashion, to the possibility, or idea, of authenticity.

In fact, nearly all the possibilities pointed to by the film are also pretty well undercut or attenuated by it. Christmas, vividly evoked with bright reds, snow and Christmas trees, is exposed as sham fairly devastatingly by Sarah Jane's materialist insistence that, since he was real, Christ must have been either black or white and by Annie (Juanita Moore) and Lora's idealist evasion in terms of it being the general idea of Christ that matters. Other possible authenticities are more ambiguously dealt with. I will look at them primarily as they relate to Lora/Turner.

The possibility of self-affirmation as a source of strength is most explored through the character of Sarah Jane (Susan Kohner) and her imitation of white, but the illusoriness of self-affirmation is underlined in the same way at certain points for both her and Lora. These ways are the use of mirror reflections at moments of affirmation and/or the introduction of the *Imitation of Life* theme on the soundtrack after such declarations. Thus when Lora rings Susie after her triumph in the role of Amy, her sense of fulfilment, achievement, is shown us only in a mirror image of it. (Compare Sarah Jane's fierce 'I'm white!' to a probing boyfriend, shown as reflected in a shop-window.)

Another possible source of authenticity is virility, here represented by Steve. Douglas Sirk often has a character like this in his films, embodying a promise of virility, to the women and impotent men of the rest of the cast – think of his use of Rock Hudson in *All That Heaven Allows*, *Written on the Wind* and *The Tarnished Angels*. The point about these characters – played by actors who are almost exaggeratedly tall, dark and handsome – is that their virility is never put to the test. They may offer the woman fulfilment (including, quite clearly, sexual fulfilment), but this remains speculative, to take place well after the end title has appeared. Sirk's films do not even end with the marriage of this male with the female protagonist, only with our assumption that this is the way all heterosexual romances end. Much less is the consummation assured. The ending of *Imitation of Life* is especially ambiguous. In one sense, it is the cobbling together of the nuclear family characteristic of the postwar film melodrama. That is to say that while we end with a nuclear family unit, it is actually made up from bits of other families (Steve is the father of neither girl; neither he nor Lora is Sarah Jane's parent). Moreover, it is shot not as father, mother and children grouped together, but as the women grouped together in the back of the car, with a cut-in shot of Steve looking on benignly from the front seat. In other words, the promise of virility that will set the seal on the family is still only a promise.

The problem with this is what exactly the film thinks of virility. Feminism has correctly exposed the oppressiveness of virility as an idea (as opposed to an idea such as energy or strength that need not be gender-specific), yet it does seem that *Imitation of Life*, and Sirk in his other films, do believe in virility as an idea. What is being critically exposed is the absence or failure of virility. In particular, the association of Steve with a certain view of the countryside (and even more a similar association between Rock Hudson and nature in *All That Heaven Allows*), seems to be presented quite straight, without undercutting, as if Sirk really believes in a natural order of virility and, possibly, the family, at least as ideals.

There is a similar problem with another of the film's alternatives to a life of imitation, namely black culture. The main lines of the Annie–Sarah Jane plot seem to be a repeat of the imitation themes in the Lora plot. The device of the black girl who can pass for white clearly demonstrates the thesis that race is a question of cultural definition, including role-playing, in which biological difference plays no significant part. Annie's investment of her self, her labour, in provision for her spectacular funeral, something which she herself by definition cannot experience, suggests the role of religious mystification in black culture. Yet the film also seems to want to say that black culture *is* more authentic than white, materially and culturally.

The role of Annie and Sarah Jane in the film is to act as the material base to the superstructure of Lora's success, which is mere phenomenal form. Annie almost lives Lora's real, practical life for her. She is the breadwinner (filling in envelopes, doing cleaning jobs, paying the bills) who enables Lora to pursue her career, and she is housewife and mother to Susie. She even at one point controls Lora's relationship with Steve, by gesturing him to go when she thinks Lora should be left alone. In other words, she is the reality, the material existence, that makes Lora's appearance possible. Moreover, it is quite clear that Lora has no conception of what it means to be black; she has no understanding of the reality that makes her life possible. She sees taking the part of the social worker as doing something more 'real' on the stage, yet cheerfully chats about its 'coloured angle' with David (Dan O'Herlihy) in front of Annie, without consulting *her*, without even seeming to register the fact that Annie is serving them drinks. When she upbraids Sarah Jane for her Southern mammy impersonation when bringing in drinks for her (Lora's) guests, she says, 'I've never treated you differently' – yet we have just seen Sarah Jane using the back stairs, going to the local school (Susie is at boarding-school), expected to help out her black servant mother. Lora has not consciously acted differently towards Sarah Jane and yet quite clearly Sarah Jane is getting different treatment. Lora has no conception of the racist structures that underpin her position and Sarah Jane's equally.

In addition to this materialist authenticity granted to blacks, the final funeral set-piece seems to affirm, its narrative significance *vis-à-vis* Annie's life notwithstanding, the cultural authenticity of blacks. Above all, the use of Mahalia Jackson (who really is Mahalia Jackson, not someone imitating her) suggests a core of real feeling in black religion. The fact that Jackson's singing is so 'genuinely' emotional that she cannot lip-synchronize herself with any precision draws attention to the artifice of the film medium which is 'unable' to 'capture' her untrammelled outpouring of emotion. Yet this final affirmation of the authenticity of black culture is also the high point of grief in the film. It is almost as if the film is saying that if there is anything other than imitation it is in suffering.

It is in relation to this that the use of Turner is most interesting, drawing as it does on both her 'artificial' and her 'suffering' image qualities. When Annie dies, Lora/Turner breaks down and cries, and it is as if some authentic feeling has broken through the hard shell of artifice elsewhere promoted by the film. It is worth comparing this with the car scene in *The Bad and the Beautiful*. In both cases, the effect is of Turner shedding her actor's artifices and giving us naked emotion. This may also be how Turner herself experienced it – we cannot know, and I do not wish to detract from her achievement in both cases. However, the effect also derives from the way both these scenes make a formal break from the rest of the film in the presentation of Turner. In *The Bad and the Beautiful*, the posed, static nature of her performance is replaced for the car scene by chaotic movement. In *Imitation of Life*, her collapse on Annie's bed makes one realize that as an element of composition everywhere else in the film, she has been used in upright and detached positions, usually still. The actual movement of falling on the bed breaks this, and the break is maintained through the funeral service where she is slumped at an angle in her seat. Whilst of course in both cases this is the art of the film-makers (of whom Turner is one) and whilst the notion of 'naked emotion' does not really have any validity, none the less this collapse into suffering, which is also a formal break in the film's compositional patterns *vis-à-vis* Turner, *means* 'authenticity', shedding of artifice, reality not imitation. What is melancholy is that this authenticity is achieved only in an image of collapse, as if the only possible reality behind the imitation of life is grief.

*

As I have been concerned in this article principally to discuss the star as an aspect of film language, I have tried generally to hold back from spelling out the ideological significance of Turner (and the star phenomenon), but a few words on this may be in order by way of a conclusion.

In this perspective the role of Turner as an agent of coherence (*Postman*) or to reinforce such notions as impulse (her marriages, *Postman*), naked emotion and authenticity (*The Bad and the Beautiful*, *Imitation of Life*) would not be viewed as progressive. At the same time, the way her image can disrupt a film text (the overall structure of *Ziegfeld Girl*, the centrality of Frank/Garfield to *Postman*) and its foregrounding of the processes of manufacture are suggestive. In a more directly political sense, it seems to me that her combination of sexuality and ordinariness was in itself ideologically explosive (and I have not sufficiently brought out the lower-class elements in this definition of ordinariness), comparable to that later embodied by Marilyn Monroe. To what extent the machinery of glamorization, punishment and suffering defused this, I'm not sure. I tend always to see ideological struggle within the texts of films, no less in Lana Turner than anywhere else.

NOTE

This chapter was originally published in 1977–8 in *Movie* 25.

1 I should like to thank Jeremy Butler for drawing my attention to a number of textual inaccuracies in the original version of this article.

REFERENCES

Alloway, Lawrence (1972) 'The iconography of the movies', in Ian Cameron (ed.) *Movie Reader*, London: November Books, 16–18.
Basinger, Jeanine (1976) *Lana Turner*, New York: Pyramid.
Cook, Jim (1977) 'On a clear day you can see forever', *Movie* 24: 61–2.
Morella, Joe and Epstein, Edward Z. (1972) *Lana: The Life and Loves of Miss Turner*, London: W. H. Allen.

FURTHER READING

Butler, Jeremy G. (ed.) (1991) *Star Texts: Image and Performance in Film and Television*, Detroit, Mich.: Wayne State University Press.
Fischer, Lucy (ed.) (1990) *Imitation of Life*, New Brunswick, NJ: Rutgers University Press.
Gledhill, Christine (ed.) (1991) *Stardom: Industry of Desire*, London: Routledge.
Kaplan, E. Ann (ed.) (1978) *Women in Film Noir*, London: British Film Institute.
Lewis, Lisa A. (ed.) (1992) *The Adoring Audience: Fan Culture and Popular Media*, London and New York: Routledge.

9 *The Son of the Sheik*

The term 'sex object' implies a certain passivity, a person just 'there' for the viewer to gaze upon. Sex objects are pinned up, fixed, to be looked at. This submissiveness accords easily with the female sex role, which is so heavily defined in terms of passivity; but what happens when it is a man who is the sex object? *The Son of the Sheik* is an interesting example of some of the ways a film can deal with having a man as the object of the camera's and the viewer's adoration.

The camera certainly does adore Valentino as Ahmed in this film. His smooth, Latin-dark skin glows like satin under the studio lighting. He is always the most important element in the composition, whether because of the way he is placed, or because of his eye-catching costumes, or because of the intensity of his movements.

In addition to this loving treatment, the film clearly sets him up as the epitome of male beauty by a sustained contrast with two other characters who are also defined by their bodies, the comically lustful dwarf and the phoney strong man at the Café Maure. Like his, their bodies are a spectacle: but whereas his is a synthesis of sexuality and strength, their bodies are grotesque parodies of one or other of these qualities. These two figures are constantly framed in relation to Ahmed, in a way that serves to heighten his sensual bodily perfection.

Such sustained sexual objectification does not mean, however, that the film contains a role reversal, with a man the object of a woman's desire in exactly the same way that, in films, women normally are of men's desires. Yasmin is seen in the film before Ahmed, and he is introduced as the object of her desire – but the way it is done is crucial. In the usual case, the male hero *sees* the woman, and there is a shot of her as he sees her – it is a shot that looks like a pin-up, like a passive object of desire. In *The Son of the Sheik*, Yasmin *thinks* about Ahmed and then there is a (flashback) shot of him – he is already located in her dreams, a spiritual realm of desire. Moreover, it is a shot of him *looking at her* dancing, looking with an eye-narrowed intensity that counteracts any notion that she might be looking at him. He is, in other words, an extremely active object of desire.

Figure 9.1 Glinting with desirability: Valentino in *The Son of the Sheik*

This goes for the whole film. He is a conventional active hero figure: his dashing adventures and swordplay are part of what makes him attractive. According to the film, female sexual desire consists of 'experiencing' a man rather than pursuing him. It is his penetrating gaze, his driving energy, that are supposed to be the turn-on, culminating in ravishment.

But it is not a rape fantasy. There is no indication that Yasmin is supposed to have enjoyed being taken by force. The morning after, there are only shots of her in tears and him looking remorseful. Rape as enjoyment of being overwhelmed may be logical conclusion of the way the film has set up women's sexual pleasure in men, but it actually holds back from that conclusion. Ahmed and Yasmin go on loving each other *despite* their violent sexual encounter, not because of it.

Ahmed's treatment of Yasmin also precipitates a row with his father, a classic Oedipal moment, a contest over the definition of correct sexual conduct. Father and son are reconciled only in the final scene, which is essentially a fight over Yasmin's honour. In between, there has been a conversation between the Sheik and his wife Diana, in which she has reminded him of his own hot-blooded ways as a youth – in *The Sheik* (1921). Just as the Sheik has grown up, so he must help his son to grow up, and the Oedipal pattern of conflict preceding the son's taking his father's place in society is repeated. This conflict between men is the real subject of the whole second half of the film, making the question of Yasmin and what she wants much less important.

The most curious aspect of the film is the relation between the setting and the characters. All act as stock Arab figures, such as sheiks and belly-dancers; and they act out a rather stark drama of sexual morality. Yet most of the main characters are not Arabs but Europeans (English and French) who live as Arabs. In this way *The Son of the Sheik* comes to feel like the 'secret life' of contemporary western society, an exploration of the then otherwise unspeakable subjects of female desire, rape and father–son conflict. The audience could take it two ways. Shocked by the sexual explicitness, it could dismiss the depicted events 'anthropologically' as foreign behaviour. Drawn into the characters, however, it could welcome the film as a sunlit dream of sexuality. In a period not yet saturated in Freudian ideas, such dreams were still possible.

NOTE

This chapter was originally published in 1982 in *The Movie* 126.

FURTHER READING

Hansen, Marion (1991) 'Pleasure, ambivalence, identification: Valentino and female spectatorship', in Christine Gledhill (ed.) *Stardom: Industry of Desire*, London: Routledge, 259–82.

10 Don't look now: the instabilities of the male pin-up

'One of the things I really envy about men,' a friend once said to me, 'is the right to look.' She went on to point out how in public places, on the street, at meetings, men could look freely at women, but that women could only look back surreptitiously, against the grain of their upbringing. It is a point that has been reiterated in many of the personal political accounts that have emerged from the consciousness-raising of the women's movement. And it is a fact that we see endlessly reworked in movies and on television. We have all seen, countless times, that scene of Young Love, where, in the canteen, at school, in church, the Boy and the Girl first see each other. The precise way it is done is very revealing. We have a close-up of him looking off camera, followed by one of her looking downwards (in a pose that has, from time immemorial, suggested maidenliness). Quite often, we move back and forth between these two close-ups, so that it is very definitely established that he looks at her and she is looked at. Then, she may look up and off camera, and we may go back briefly to the boy still looking – but it is only briefly, for no sooner is it established that she sees him than we must be assured that she at once averts her eyes. She has seen him, but she doesn't look at him as he looks at her – having seen him, she quickly resumes being the one who is looked at.

So utterly routine is this kind of scene that we probably don't remark on it, yet it encapsulates, and effectively reinforces, one of the fundamental ways by which power relations between the sexes are maintained. In her book *Body Politics*, Nancy M. Henley examines the very many different non-verbal ways that gender roles and male power are constantly being rebuilt and reaffirmed. She does for gesture, body posture, facial expressions and so on what, most recently, Dale Spender's *Man Made Language* does for verbal communication, and shows how non-verbal communication is both a register of male–female relations and one of the means by which those relations are kept the way they are. Particularly relevant here is her discussion of eye contact.

Henley argues that it is not so much a question of whether women or men look at each other, but how they do. In fact, her evidence suggests that in face-to-face interactions, women look at men more than men do at women – but then this is because women listen more to men, pay more attention to them. In other words, women do not so much look at men as watch them. On the other hand, in crowd situations, men look more at women – men stare at women, whereas women avert their eyes. In both cases, this (re-)establishes male dominance. In the first case (one-to-one), 'superior position . . . is communicated by visually ignoring the other person – *not* looking while listening, but looking into space as if the other isn't there'; whereas in the second case (crowds), 'staring is used to *assert* dominance – to establish, to maintain, and to regain it' (1977: 166).

Images of men aimed at women – whether star portraits, pin-ups, or drawings and paintings of men – are in a particularly interesting relation to these eye contact patterns. A certain instability is produced – the first of several we encounter when looking at images of men that are offered as sexual spectacle. On the one hand, this is a visual medium, these men are there to be looked at by women. On the other hand, this does violence to the codes of who looks and who is looked at (and how), and some attempt is instinctively made to counteract this violation. Much of this centres on the model or star's own 'look' – where and how he is looking in relation to the woman looking at him, in the audience or as she leafs through the fan or women's magazine (not only *Playgirl*, which has male nudes as *Playboy* has female ones, but also the new teenage magazines like *Oh Boy!* and *My Guy*, with their half-dressed pin-ups, and such features as 'Your Daily Male' in the *Sun* and 'She-Male' in *She*) (Figure 10.1).

To repeat, it is not a question of whether or not the model looks at his spectator(s), but how he does or does not. In the case of not looking, where the female model typically averts her eyes, expressing modesty, patience and a lack of interest in anything else, the male model looks either off or up. In the case of the former (Figure 10.2), his look suggests an interest in something else that the viewer cannot see – it certainly doesn't suggest any interest in the viewer. Indeed, it barely acknowledges the viewer, whereas the woman's averted eyes do just that – they are averted from the viewer. In the cases where the model is looking up, this always suggests a spirituality (Figure 10.3): he might be there for his face and body to be gazed at, but his mind is on higher things, and it is this upward striving that is most supposed to please. This pose encapsulates the kind of dualism that Paul Hoch analyses in his study of masculinity, *White Hero, Black Beast* – higher is better than lower, the head above is better than the genitals below. At the same time, the sense of straining and striving upwards does also suggest analogies with the definition of the very sexuality supposedly relegated to an inferior place – straining and striving are the terms most often used to describe male sexuality in this society.

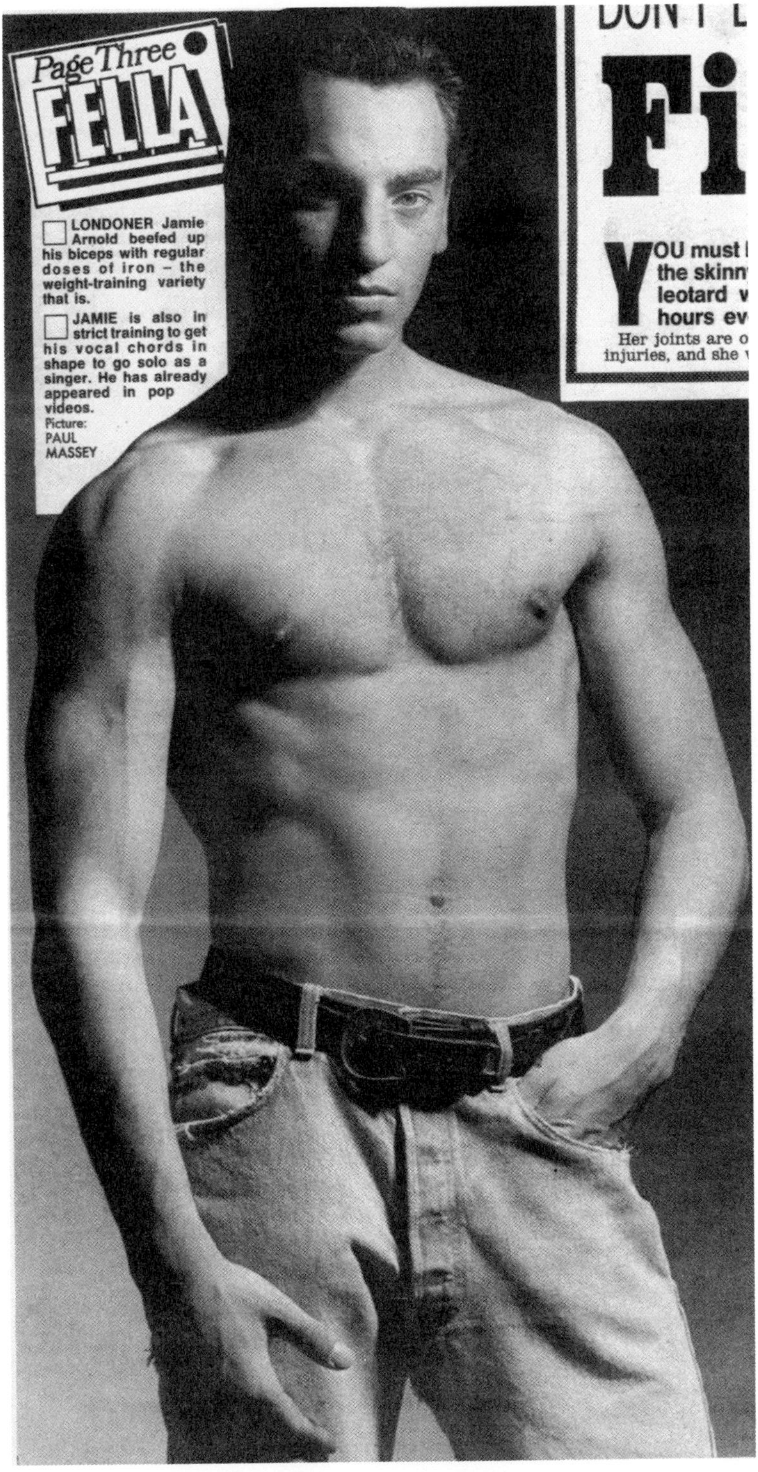

Figure 10.1 'Mirror Fella', 11 January 1990

Figure 10.2 Looking off: Rudolph Valentino

Figure 10.3 Looking up: Montgomery Clift

Figure 10.4 Looking through: Paul Newman

It may be, as is often said, that male pin-ups more often than not do not look at the viewer, but it is by no means the case that they never do. When they do, what is crucial is the kind of look it is, something very often determined by the set of the mouth that accompanies it. When the female pin-up returns the viewer's gaze, it is usually some kind of smile, inviting. The male pin-up, even at his most benign, still stares at the viewer. Even Paul Newman's frank face-on to the camera (Figure 10.4) or the *Oh Boy!* coverboy's yearning gaze at us still seems to reach beyond the boundary marked, when the photo was taken, by the camera, as if he wants to reach beyond and through and establish himself. The female model's gaze stops at that boundary, the male's looks right through it.

Freud noticed a similar sort of look on Michelangelo's statue of Moses – though Moses is not looking at us but at the Jews' worship of the Golden Calf. Since Freud, it is common to describe such a look as 'castrating' or 'penetrating' – yet to use such words to describe the look of a man at a woman is revealing in ways that Freudians do not always intend. What, after all, have women to fear from the threat of castration? And why, come to that, should the possibility of penetration be *necessarily* fearful to women? It is clear that castration can only be a threat to men, and more probable that it is the taboo of male anal eroticism that causes masculine-defined men to construct penetration as frightening and the concept of male (hetero)sexuality as 'taking' a woman that constructs penetration as an act of violence. In looking at and dealing with these castrating/penetrating looks, women are caught up in a system that does not so much address them as work out aspects of the construction of male sexuality in men's heads.

If the first instability of the male pin-up is the contradiction between the fact of being looked at and the attempt of the model's look to deny it, the second is the apparent address to women's sexuality and the actual working out of male sexuality (and this may be one of the reasons why male pin-ups notoriously don't 'work' for women). What is at stake is not just male and female sexuality, but male and female power. The maintenance of power underpins further instabilities in the image of men as sexual spectacle, in terms of the active/passive nexus of looking, the emphasis on muscularity and the symbolic association of male power and the phallus.

The idea of looking (staring) as power and being looked at as powerlessness overlaps with ideas of activity/passivity. Thus to look is thought of as active; whereas to be looked at is passive. In reality, this is not true. The model prepares her or himself to be looked at, the artist or photographer constructs the image to be looked at; and, on the other hand, the image that the viewer looks at is not summoned up by his or her act of looking but in collaboration with those who have put the image there. Most of us probably experience looking and being looked at, in life as in art, somewhere among these shifting relations of activity and passivity. Yet it remains the case that images of men must disavow this element of passivity if they are to be kept in line with dominant ideas of masculinity-as-activity.

For this reason images of men are often images of men doing something. When, before the full invention of cinematography, Eadweard Muybridge took an enormous series of photographic sequences, each one in the sequence taken a few seconds after the other, one of his intentions was to study the nature of movement. Muybridge photographed sequences of naked male and female figures. In a study of these sequences, Linda Williams (1981) shows how, even in so 'scientific' an undertaking and at such a comparatively 'primitive' stage in the development of photography, Muybridge established a difference between the female subjects, who are just there to be looked at, and the male subjects, who are doing something (carrying a boulder, sawing wood, playing baseball) which we can look in on. This distinction is maintained in the history of the pin-up, where time and again the image of the man is one caught in the middle of an action, or associated, through images in the pictures, with activity.

Even when not actually caught in an act, the male image still promises activity by the way the body is posed. Even in an apparently relaxed, supine pose, the model tightens and tautens his body so that the muscles are emphasized, hence drawing attention to the body's potential for action (Figure 10.5). More often, the male pin-up is not supine anyhow, but standing taut ready for action.

There is an interesting divergence here in ethnic and class terms, a good example of the way that images of male power are always and necessarily inflected with other aspects of power in society. In relation to ethnicity, it is generally the case that the activity shown or implied in images of white men is clearly related to the split in western society between leisure and work activity, whereas black men, even though they are in fact American or European, are given a physicality that is inextricably linked to notions of 'the jungle', and hence 'savagery'. This is done either by a natural setting, in which a generalized physical exertion is conflated with the energies of nature (and, doubtless, the beat of drums), or else, more recently, in the striking use of 'black power' symbolism (Figure 10.6). This might seem like an acknowledgement of ethnic politics, and perhaps for some viewers it is, but the way the media constructed black power in fact tended to reproduce the idea of a savage energy rather than a political movement – hence the stress on back-to-Africa (in the white western imagination still an amorphous jungle), or the 'senseless' violence erupting from the jungle of the ghetto.

Such images also put black men 'outside of' class (though there has been the promotion of specifically middle-class black images, as with,

Figure 10.5 Supine but taut for *Playgirl*

Figure 10.6 Black power as sex appeal: Billy Dee Williams

Figure 10.7 Bodybuilding and the Third World: *Arnold Schwarzenegger*

especially, Sidney Poitier). White men are more likely to be class differentiated, but this does overlap with the work/leisure distinction. Work is in fact almost suppressed from dominant imagery in this society – it is mainly in socialist imagery that its images occur. In nineteenth-century socialist and trade union art and in Soviet socialist realism the notions of the dignity and heroism of labour are expressed through dynamically muscular male bodies. As Eric Hobsbawm (1978) has pointed out, what this tradition has done, in effect, is to secure for masculinity the definition of what is finest in the proletarian and socialist traditions – women have been marginalized to the ethereal role of 'inspiration'. Moreover, it is certainly no *conscious* part of this tradition that these male bodies should be a source of erotic visual pleasure, for men and women.

Sport is the area of life that is the most common contemporary source of male imagery – not only in pin-ups of sportsmen, but in the sports activities of film stars, pop stars and so on. (*She* magazine has run a series of pin-ups of wrestlers.) Although certain sports have very clear class associations (the Prince of Wales plays polo, not football), there is a sense in which sport is a 'leveller'. Running, swimming, ball games are pretty well open to anyone in any class, and so imagery derived from these activities does not have immediate class associations. What all imply, however, is leisure, and the strength and vitality to use it. The celebration of the body in sport is also a celebration of the relative affluence of western society, where people have time to dedicate themselves to the development of the body for its own sake.

Whether the emphasis is on work or sport or any other activity, the body quality that is promoted is muscularity. In the copy accompanying the pin-ups in *Oh Boy!*, for instance, the female readers are called on to 'getta load of his muscles' and other such invitations. Although the hyper-developed muscularity of an Arnold Schwarzenegger is regarded by most people as excessive, and perhaps bordering on the fascist (Figure 10.7), it is still the case that muscularity is a key term in appraising men's bodies. This again probably comes from men themselves. Muscularity is the *sign* of power – natural, achieved, phallic.

At a minimum, developed muscles indicate a physical strength that women do not generally match (although recent developments in women's sport and physical conditioning suggest that differences between the sexes here may not be so fixed). The potential for muscularity in men is seen as a biological given, and is also the means of dominating both women and other men who are in the competition for the spoils of the earth – and women. The point is that muscles are biological, hence 'natural', and we persist in habits of thought, especially in the area of sexuality and gender, whereby what can be shown to be natural must be accepted as given and inevitable. The 'naturalness' of muscles legitimizes male power and domination (Figure 10.8).

However, developed muscularity – muscles that *show* – is not in truth

Figure 10.8 Muscles and the naturalization of male power in *Viva* for women

natural at all, but is rather achieved. The muscle man is the end-product of his own activity of muscle-building. As always, the comparison with the female body beautiful is revealing. Rationally, we know that the beauty queen has dieted, exercised, used cleansing creams, solariums and cosmetics – but none of this really shows in her appearance, and is anyway generally construed as something that has been *done to* the woman. Conversely, a man's muscles constantly bespeak this achievement of his beauty/power.

Muscles, as well as being a sign of activity and achievement, are hard. We've already seen how even not overly developed male pin-ups harden their bodies to be looked at. This hardness may then be reinforced by aspects of setting or symbolic references, or by poses that emphasize hard lines and angular shapes (not the soft roundness of the feminine aesthetic). In her book *The Nude Male*, Margaret Walters suggests this hardness is phallic, not in the direct sense of being like an erect penis but rather in being symbolic of all that the phallus represents of 'abstract paternal power'. There is no doubt that the image of the phallus as power is widespread to the point of near-universality, all the way from tribal and early Greek fertility symbols to the language of pornography, where the penis is endlessly described as a weapon, a tool, a source of terrifying power.

There is a danger of casual thought here. The phallus is not just an arbitrarily chosen symbol of male power; it is crucial that the penis has provided the model for this symbol. Because only men have penises, phallic symbols, even if in some sense possessed by a woman (as may be the case with female rulers, for instance), are always symbols of ultimately male power. The woman who wields 'phallic' power does so in the interests of men.

This leads to the greatest instability of all for the male image. For the fact is that the penis isn't a patch on the phallus. The penis can never live up to the mystique implied by the phallus. Hence the excessive, even hysterical quality of so much male imagery. The clenched fists, the bulging muscles, the hardened jaws, the proliferation of phallic symbols – they are all straining after what can hardly ever be achieved, the embodiment of the phallic mystique (Figure 10.9). This is even more the case with the male nude. The limp penis can never match up to the mystique that has kept it hidden from view for the last couple of centuries, and even the erect penis often looks awkward, stuck on to the man's body as if it is not a part of him (Figure 10:10).

Like so much else about masculinity, images of men, founded on such multiple instabilities, are such a strain. Looked at but pretending not to be, still yet asserting movement, phallic but weedy – there is seldom anything easy about such imagery. And the real trap at the heart of these instabilities is that it is precisely *straining* that is held to be the great good, what makes a man a man. Whether head held high reaching up

Figure 10.9 Hysterical iconography: Humphrey Bogart 'at home'

Figure 10.10 Looking awkward for *Playgirl*

for an impossible transcendence or penis jerking up in a hopeless assertion of phallic mastery, men and women alike are asked to value the very things that make masculinity such an unsatisfactory definition of being human.

NOTE

This chapter was originally published in 1982 in *Screen* 23 (3–4).

REFERENCES

Henley, Nancy M. (1977) *Body Politics*, Englewood Cliffs, NJ: Prentice-Hall.

Hobsbawm, Eric (1978) 'Man and woman in socialist iconography', *History Workshop Journal* 6: 121–38.

Hoch, Paul (1979) *White Hero, Black Beast*, London: Pluto Press.

Spender, Dale (1980) *Man Made Language*, London: Routledge & Kegan Paul.

Walters, Margaret (1978) *The Nude Male*, London: Paddington Press.

Williams, Linda (1981) 'Film body: an implantation of perversions', *Cinétracts* 3 (4): 19–35.

FURTHER READING

Brauerhoch, Annette (1986) 'Glanz und elend der muskelmänner', *Frauen und Film* 40: 20–6.

Cooper, Emmanuel (1989) *The Sexual Perspective*, London: Routledge & Kegan Paul.

Green, Ian (1984) 'Malefunction', *Screen* 25 (4–5): 36–49.

Kent, Sarah (1985) 'The erotic male nude', in Sarah Kent and Jacqueline Morreau (eds) *Women's Images of Men*, London: Writers & Readers Publishing, 75–105.

Mercer, Kobena and Julien, Isaac (1988) 'Race, sexual politics and black masculinity', in Rowena Chapman and Jonathan Rutherford (eds) *Male Order*, London: Lawrence & Wishart, 97–164.

Moore, Suzanne (1988) 'Here's looking at you, kid!', in Lorraine Gamman and Margaret Marshment (eds) *The Female Gaze*, London: Women's Press, 44–59.

Neale, Steve (1983) 'Masculinity as spectacle', *Screen* 24 (6): 2–16.

Waugh, Thomas (1984) 'Photography, passion and power', *The Body Politic* 101: 29–33.

11 Coming to terms: gay pornography

The main suggestions I'd like to make in this essay about gay male pornographic cinema are quite brief and simple. Broadly I'm going to argue that the narrative structure of gay porn[1] is analogous to aspects of the social construction of both male sexuality in general and gay male sexual practice in particular. But before getting on to that it seems necessary to say a few things by way of introduction. Pornography has recently become a Big Topic in left cultural work,[2] and what I'm going to say needs to be situated in relation to this.

First, a definition – a working definition, the one I'm going to be working with here, rather than a statement of the correct definition of pornography. I want some definition that is as broadly descriptive as possible. Discussion about porn tends to start off by being either for or against all porn and to be caught up in equally dubious libertarian or puritanical ideas. I don't mean to imply that I believe in the myth of objectivity, that I start off utterly neutral. I'm a gay man, who has (unlike women) easy access to porn and can take pleasure in it,[3] but who feels a commitment to the more feminist inflections of gay male politics. I'm also a socialist who sees porn as capitalist production but does not believe all capitalist cultural production always all the time expresses capitalist ideology (cf. Lovell 1980). I'm constantly looking for moments of contradiction, instability and give in our culture, the points at which change can be effected, and want to start out with the possibility of finding it in porn as anywhere else. So the definition I'm going to use is that a pornographic film is *any* film that has as its aim sexual arousal in the spectator.

This definition makes porn film a familiar kind of genre, that is, one that is based on the effect that both producers and audiences know the film is supposed to have. It is not defined (or I am not asking to define it here), like the Western, gangster film, or musical, by such aesthetic, textual elements as iconography, structure, style and so on, but by what it produces in the spectator. It is like genres such as the weepie and the thriller, and also low or vulgar comedy. Like all of these, it is supposed to have an effect that is registered in the spectator's body – s/he weeps, gets goose-bumps, rolls about laughing, comes. Like these genres, porn is usually discussed in relation to a similar, but 'higher' genre which doesn't have a bodily effect – weepies (melodramas and soap opera) are compared to tragedy or realist drama, thrillers to mystery/detective stories (based on intellectual, puzzle-solving narratives), low comedy (farce) to high comedy (comedy of manners), and porn to erotica.

I'd like to use porn as a neutral term, describing a particular genre. If one defines porn differently, then the kind of defence of porn as a genre (but emphatically not of most porn that is actually available) that I'm involved with here is not really possible. Current feminist critiques of pornography (e.g. Dworkin 1981, Griffin 1981, Lederer 1980) rightly stress the degradation of women that characterizes so much heterosexual porn, and these critiques in fact define pornography as woman-degrading representations of sexuality. Although feeling closer to some of those feminist articles that take issue with this hardline anti-porn position (Myers 1982, Allen and Harris 1982, Winship 1982, Rich 1982), I do not feel as out of sympathy with, say, Andrea Dworkin's work as many people, and especially gay men, that I know. Although in relation to gay porn Dworkin is in some respects inaccurate (e.g. in stressing gay porn's use of socially inferior – young, black – men in 'feminine' positions, whereas similarity between partners is more often the case) or out of date (Allen and Harris 1982: 22), her rage at what so much of porn consists of is fully justified, and especially so because she effectively defines porn as that which is degrading and out*rage*ous. But I'd like all the same to hang on to a wider notion of sexual representation, and still use the word pornography precisely because of its disreputable, carnal associations. (Maybe the feminist debate means that I can't use the word like this – but I don't want to fall for the trap of substituting the word erotica.[4])

The fact that porn, like weepies, thrillers and low comedy, is realized in/through the body has given it low status in our culture. Popularity these genres have, but arbiters of cultural status still tend to value 'spiritual' over 'bodily' qualities, and hence relegate porn and the rest to an inferior cultural position.

One of the results of this is that culturally validated knowledge of the body, of the body's involvement in emotion, tends to be intellectual knowledge about the body, uninformed by experiential knowledge of it.[5] Let me try to be clear about this. I'm not saying that there can be a transparent, pure knowledge of the body, untouched by historical and cultural reality. On the contrary, all knowledge is culturally and historically specific, we do not transcend our material circumstances. We learn to feel our bodies in particular ways, not 'naturally'. But an intellectual or spiritual knowledge about the body is different from experiential knowledge of the body – both are socially constructed, but the latter is always in a dynamic material and physical relationship with the body, is always knowledge in and of the body. Intellectual or spiritual knowledge on the other hand divorces social construction from that which it constructs, divorces knowledge about the body from knowing with the body. (Certain types of discourse analysis – but by no means all – clearly fall into the same idealist trap.[6])

Moreover, the effect of the cultural status of intellectual/spiritual accounts of the body is to relegate experiential knowledge of the body to a residual category. Of course idealist discourse accounts do not allow any such category at all.[7] Thus experiential knowledge (except when sanctified by the subjugation of the body in most forms of 'physical education') is allowed to be both inferior and just a given, not socially constructed,[8] to be just 'experience', not socially constructed experiential knowledge. By valuing the spiritual, the bodily is left as something natural, and sexuality as the most natural thing of all. What is in fact also socially constructed (experiential knowledge of the body, and of sexuality) is not recognized as such, and for that reason is not reflected upon, is allowed to go its supposed own way until it meets up with spiritual censors. Even gay theory and feminist theory have been notoriously reluctant to think through the social construction of the body without lapsing into the Scylla of Lacanian psychoanalysis (where social construction does not construct anything *out of* any material reality) and the Charybdis of both gay liberationist let-it-all-hang-out (where sexuality is a pure impulse awaiting release) and the implicit sexual essentialism of radical feminist ideas of masculine aggression and women's power (cf. Wilson 1983).

A defence of porn as a genre (which, I repeat, is not at all the same thing as defending most of what porn currently consists of) would be based on the idea that an art rooted in bodily effect can give us a knowledge of the body that other art cannot.

Even now porn does give us knowledge of the body – only it is mainly bad knowledge, reinforcing the worst aspects of the social construction of masculinity that men learn to experience in our bodies. All the same, porn can be a site for 're-educating desire' (Carter 1981) and in a way that constructs desire in the body, not merely theoretically in relation to, and often against, it.

To do that, though, means rejecting any notion of 'pure sex', and particularly the defence of porn as expressing or releasing a sexuality 'repressed' by bourgeois (etc.) society. This argument has gained some ground in gay male circles, and with good reason. Homosexual desire has been constructed as perverse and unspeakable; gay porn does speak/show gay sex. Gay porn asserts homosexual desire, it turns the definition of homosexual desire on its head, says bad is good, sick is healthy and so on. It thus defends the universal human practice of same sex physical contact (which our society constructs as homosexual); it has made life bearable for countless millions of gay men.

But to move from there to suggest that what we have here is a natural sexuality bursting out of the confines of heterosexual artificial repression is much more of a problem.

This is certainly the way that Gregg Blachford's article 'Looking at pornography' (1988) can be read, and seems to be the contention behind David Ehrenstein's article 'Within the pleasure principle, or irresponsible homosexual propaganda' (1980). The latter[9] argues that porn movies, unlike mainstream films that imply sexuality but don't show it, give us the pure pleasure of voyeurism which lies unacknowledged behind all cinema.

> The pornographic is obvious, absolute, unmistakable – no lies or omissions or evasions can hold quarter in its sphere.

Porn is the 'abandon of everything to the pleasure principle' (ibid.: 65) conceptualized as pure drive (the more usual appropriation of Freudian ideas than the Lacanian version influential in academic film studies circles). Porn itself operates with this idea, and the view is clearly expressed in the introduction to *Meat* (McDonald 1981), a collection of writings from the magazine *Straight to Hell*. The magazine, like the book, consists entirely of personal accounts of gay sexual experience sent in to the magazine by gay men. I have no reason to suppose that the accounts are not genuine both in the sense of having actually been sent in (not ghost-written) and of describing real experiences. But this 'genuineness' is not to be conflated, as book and magazine do, with the notion of an unconstructed sexuality – raw, pure and so on. A reading of *Meat*, or a look at gay porn, indicates really rather obviously that the sexuality described/represented is socially meaningful. Class, ethnicity and of course concepts of masculinity and gayness/straightness all clearly mark these gay pornographic productions: and indeed the very stress on sexuality as a moment of truth, and its conceptualization as raw, pure, etc., is itself historically and culturally produced (Foucault 1980).

What makes *Meat* and gay movie-house porn especially interesting and important is the extent to which they blur the line between representation and practice. *Meat* is based on (I think largely) true encounters that really happened. Watching porn in gay cinemas usually involves having sex as well – not just self-masturbation but sexual activity with others, in a scenario brilliantly evoked by Will Aitken (1981–2) in his article 'Erect in the dark'. In principle then gay porn is a form of representation that can be the site and occasion for the production of bodily knowledge of the body. In this definition, porn is too important to be ignored, or to be left to the pornographers.

NARRATIVE MANIFESTATION

I'd like now to turn to one of the ways in which the education of desire that porn is involved in is manifested, namely its use of narrative[10].

It is often said that porn movies as a genre are characterized by their absence of narrative. The typical porn movie, hard core anyway, is held to be an endless series of people fucking, and not even, as Beatrice Faust notes, fucking in the 'normal' physiological order that Masters and Johnson have 'recorded' (1982: 16). Gay porn (and indeed what hetero porn I have seen), however, is full of narrative. Narrative is its very basis.

Even the simplest pornographic loops have narrative. In those quarter-in-the-slot machines where you just get a bit of a porn loop for your quarter, you are very conscious of what point (roughly) you have come into the loop, you are conscious of where the narrative has got to. Even if all that is involved is a fuck between two men, there are the following narrative elements: the arrival on the scene of the fuck, establishing contact (through greeting and recognition, or through a quickly established eye-contact agreement to fuck), undressing, exploring various parts of the body, coming, parting. The exploration of the body often involves exploring those areas less heavily codified in terms of sexuality, before 'really getting down to/on with' those that are (genitals and anus). Few short porn films don't involve most or all of these narrative elements, and in that order. Usually too there is some sort of narrative detail – in *Muscle Beach* (Figure 11.1), one man (Rick Wolfmier) arrives on the scene (a beach) in a truck, the other man (Mike Betts) is already there sunbathing; Wolfmier walks by the sea for a while; there is quite a long sequence of shot:reverse shot cutting as they see each other and establish contact; self-masturbation precedes their actual physical contact with each other; after orgasm, Wolfmier and Betts drive away together in the truck. Already then minimal character elements are present, of not inconsiderable social interest – the iconography of the truck, the looks of the two men, the culture of the beach and of body-building, and so on.

Even when the film is yet more minimal than this, there is still narrative – and essentially the same narrative, too. Some gay porn loops simply show one man masturbating. A rather stylish version of this is *Roger*, which just has the eponymous star masturbating. The music is a kind of echoing drumbeat; there is no set to speak of; the lighting is red, covering the screen in varieties of pulsating hue; the film cuts between long shots and medium shots in a quite rhythmic way, often dissolving rather than cutting clean. It will be clear that there is something almost abstract or avant-gardeish about the film, as the cinematic means play visually with its solo subject, Roger masturbating. Yet even here there is a basic narrative – Roger enters, masturbates, comes. (Where you put

Figure 11.1 Bodybuilding and romance: *Muscle Beach*

your quarter in might mean that *you* start with his orgasm and run on to where he comes in; but you'd know and be able to reconstruct the proper narrative order that your quarter has cut across.)

Even in so minimal and abstract a case, there is narrative – *Roger* is a classic goal-directed narrative. The desire that drives the porn narrative forward is the desire to come, to have an orgasm. And it seems to me that male sexuality, homo or hetero, is socially constructed, at the level of representation anyway, in terms of narrative; that, as it were, male sexuality is itself understood narratively.

The goal of the pornographic narrative is coming; in filmic terms, the goal is ejaculation, that is, visible coming. If the goal of the pornographic protagonist (the actor or 'character') is to come, the goal of the spectator is to see him come (and, more often than not, to come at the same time as him). Partly this has to do with 'proof', with the form's 'literalness', as Beatrice Faust puts it, with the idea that if you don't really see semen the performer could have faked it (and so you haven't had value for money). But partly too it has to do with the importance of the visual in the way male sexuality is constructed/conceptualized. It is striking how much pornographic literature, not a visual medium, stresses the visible elements of sex. (Most remarkable perhaps is Walter, the Victorian narrator of *My Secret Life*, with his obsessive desire to see into his partner's vagina, even to the detail of seeing, for instance, what his semen looks like after he has ejaculated it into her vagina.) Men's descriptions of their own erections seldom have to do with how their penises feel, but with how they look. The emphasis on seeing orgasm is then part of the way porn (re)produces the construction of male sexuality.

Could it be otherwise, could sexuality be represented differently? So dominant are masculine-centred definitions of sexuality that it often seems as if all representations of sexuality (pornographic or otherwise) are constructed as driven narrative. But there are alternatives, and one that struck me was the lesbian sequence at the end of *Je tu il elle*, directed by Chantal Akerman. (As Margaret Mead pointed out, you need only one example of things being different to establish that things can be different in the organization of human existence and hence that things can be changed.) The sequence itself is part of a (minimalist) narrative; but taken by itself it does not have the narrative drive of male porn. It starts *in media res* – there is no arrival in the room, the women are already making love when the sequence starts (though the previous shot has, perhaps ambiguously, established that they are going to make love); there is no sense of a progression to the goal of orgasm; nor is there any attempt to find visual or even (as in hetero porn?) aural equivalents for the visible male ejaculation. In particular, there is no sense of genital activity being the last, and getting-down-to-the-real-thing, stage of the experience. It is done in three long takes – no editing cuts across a sexual narrative (as in gay porn; see below); the harsh white lighting and the women's white bodies on crumpled white sheets in a room painted white, contribute to the effect of representing the sexuality as more dissolving and ebbing than a masculine thrusting narrative. Let me stress that I am *not* talking about what the women are doing – for much of the time their actions are far more snatching and grabbing than, for instance, the generally smooth, wet action of fellatio in gay porn. My point is the difference in narrative organization, in the cinematic representation of sexuality.[11]

I am not suggesting that this is a better representation of sexuality, or the correct mode for representing lesbian sexuality. Also I want to bracket the question of whether the difference between the two modes of representation is based on biological differences between female and male sexuality, or on different social constructions of sexuality, or on a combination of the two.[12] All I want to get over is the difference itself, and the fact that male porn, whether homo or hetero, is ineluctably caught in the narrative model. (This is particularly significant in hetero porn in that it is predominantly constructed around a female protagonist (Giles 1976), who is attributed with this narrativized sexuality. However, I am not about to get into whether this is a gain – a recognition of female sexuality as desire – or a loss – a construction of female sexuality in male terms.)

The basis of gay porn film is a narrative sexuality, a construction of male sexuality as the desire to achieve the goal of a visual climax. In relation to gay sexual politics, it is worth signalling that this should give pause to those of us who thought/hoped that being a gay man meant that we were breaking with the gender role system. At certain levels this is true, but there seems no evidence that in the predominant form of how we represent our sexuality to ourselves (in gay porn) we in any way break from the norms of male sexuality.

Particularly significant here is the fact that although the pleasure of anal sex (that is, of being anally fucked) is represented, the narrative is never organized around the desire to be fucked, but around the desire to ejaculate (whether or not following on from anal intercourse). Thus although at the level of public representation gay men may be thought of as deviant and disruptive of masculine norms because we assert the pleasures of being fucked and the eroticism of the anus (Hocquenghem 1978), in our pornography this takes a back seat.[13]

This is why porn is politically important. Gay porn, like much of the gay male ghetto, has developed partly out of the opening up of social spaces achieved by the gay liberation movements; but porn and the ghetto have overwhelmingly developed within the terms of masculinity. The knowledge that gay porn (re)produces must be put together with the fact that gay men (like straight men but unlike women) do have this mode of public sexual expression available to them, however debased it may be. Like male homosexuality itself, gay porn is always in this very ambiguous relationship to male power and privilege, neither fully within it nor fully outside it (cf. Barrett 1980: 42–84, *passim*). But that ambiguity is a contradiction that can be exploited. In so far as porn is part of the experiential education of the body, it has contributed to and legitimized the masculine model of gay sexuality, a model that always implies the subordination of women. But rather than just allowing it to carry on doing so, it should be our concern to work against *this* pornography by working with/within pornography to change it – either by interventions within pornographic film-making itself (Siebenand 1980), or by the development of porn within the counter-cinemas (always remembering that the distinction between porn in the usual commercial sense and sexual underground/alternative/independent cinema has always been blurry when you come to look at the films themselves), or by criticism that involves audiences reflecting on their experience of pornography (rather than by closing down on reflection by straight condemnation or celebration of it).

So far all I've been talking about is the most basic, minimal narrative organization of (gay) male pornography. However, gay porn is characterized as much by the elaborations of its narrative method as by its insistence on narrative itself. Though the bare narrative elements may often not go beyond those described above, they are frequently organized into really quite complex narrative wholes. Often there is a central narrative thread – two men who are in love or who want to get off with each other – but this is punctuated by almost all of the devices of narrative elaboration imaginable, most notably flashbacks (to other encounters, or previous encounters of the main characters with each other), fantasies (again, with others or each other, of what might or could be), parallelism (cutting back and forth between two or more different sexual encounters) and so on. All preserve the coming-to-visual-climax underlying narrative organization, but why this fascination with highly wrought narrative patterns? To begin with, of course, it is a way of getting more fucks in, with more people (Mele and Thirkell 1981). There is even perhaps an element of humour, as the film-makers knowingly strain their imagination to think of ways of bringing in yet more sex acts. But it is also a way of teasing the audience sexually, because it is a way of delaying climax, of extending foreplay. In parallel sequences, each fuck is effectively temporally extended, each climax is delayed. More generally, the various additional encounters delay the fulfilment of the basic narrative of the two men who are the central characters. (For example, in *L.A. Tool and Die* the underlying narrative is Wylie's journey to Los Angeles to find a job and his lover Hank; Wylie and Hank are played by the stars of the film, Will Seagers and Richard Locke, so we know that their having sex together must be the climax; but there are various encounters along Wylie's way, including memories, observation of other couples, incidental encounters with other men, and even inserted scenes with characters with whom Wylie has no connection, before arrival at Los Angeles and finally making it with Hank.)

There is a third reason for this narrative elaboration. Just as the minimal coming-to-visual-climax structure is a structural analogue for male sexuality, so the effective multiplication of sex acts through elaborate narrativity is an analogue for a (utopian) model of a gay sexual life-style that combines a basic romanticism with an easy acceptance of promiscuity. Thus the underlying narrative is often romantic, the ultimate goal is to make love with *the* man; but along the way a free-ranging, easy-going promiscuity is possible. While not all gay men actually operate such a model of how they wish to organize their affective lives, it is a very predominant one in gay cultural production, a utopian reconciliation of the desire for romance *and* promiscuity, security *and* freedom, making love *and* having sex.

It is worth stressing how strong the element of romance is, since this is perhaps less expected than the celebration of promiscuity. The plot of *L.A. Tool and Die* outlined above is a good example, as is *Navy Blue* in which two sailors on shore leave seek out other lovers because each doesn't think that the other is gay, yet each is really in love with the other (as fantasy sequences make clear) – only at the end of the film do they realize their love for each other. Or take *Wanted*, a gay porn version of *The Defiant Ones*, in which two convicts, one gay (Al Parker) and one straight (Will Seagers), escape from prison together. Despite Seagers's hostility to Parker's sexuality, they stick together, with Parker having various sexual encounters, including watching Seagers masturbate. The film is a progression from the sadistic prison sexuality at the start (also offered, I know, as pornographic pleasure), through friendly mutual sexual pleasuring between Parker and various other men, to a final encounter, by an idyllic brookside, between Parker and Seagers which is the culmination of their developing friendship. Some men I know who've seen the film find this final sequence too conventionally romantic (which it is – that's why I like it) or else too bound up with the self-oppressive fantasy of the straight man who deigns to have sex with a fag. It can certainly be taken that way, but I know when I first saw it I was really moved by what seemed to be Seagers's realization of the sexuality of his feeling for Parker. And what particularly moved me was the moment when Seagers comes in Parker's mouth, and the latter gently licks the semen off Seagers's penis, because here it seemed was an explicit and arousing moment of genital sexuality that itself expressed a tender emotional feeling – through its place in the narrative, through the romanticism of the setting, through the delicacy of Parker's performance. If porn taught us *this* more often . . .

One of the most interesting ways of making narratives complex in gay porn is the use of films within films. Many gay pron films are about making gay porn films, and many others involve someone showing gay porn films to himself or someone else (with the film-within-the-film then becoming for a while the film we are watching). The process of watching, and also of being watched (in the case of those films about making gay porn) is thus emphasized, not in the interests of foregrounding the means of construction in order to deconstruct them, but because the pleasure of seeing sex is what motivates (gay) male pornography and can be heightened by having attention drawn to it. (There is a whole other topic, to do with the power in play in looking/being looked at, which I won't get into here.) We have in these cases a most complex set of relations between screen and auditorium. On screen someone actually having sex is watched (photographed) by a film-maker watched (photographed) by another invisible film-maker (the one who made the film on screen), and all are watched by someone in the audience who is (or generally reckons to be) himself actually having sex. Gay porn here collapses the distinction between representation and that which it is a representation of, while at the same time showing very clearly the degree to which representation is part of the pleasure to be had even in that which it is a representation of. Porn (all porn) is, for good or ill (and currently mainly for ill), part of how we live our sexuality; how we represent sexuality to ourselves is part of how we live it, and porn has rather cornered the market on the representation of sexuality. Gay porn seems to make that all the clearer, because there is greater equality between the participants (performers, film-makers, audiences)[14] which permits a fuller exploration of the education of desire that is going on. Porn involves us bodily in that education: criticism of porn should be opening up reflection on the education we are receiving in order to change it.

ACKNOWLEDGEMENT

I'd like to thank *Jump Cut* editorial collective for their helpful and also very enjoyable involvement in the editing of this article. Since first writing it I have incorporated not only many of their suggestions but also much of the useful discussion on pornography and gay macho in the Birmingham Gay Men's Socialist Group. Many thanks to all these people, then – but I'll still take the blame for the finished article.

NOTES

This chapter was originally published in 1985 in *Jump Cut* 30.

1 For the rest of the article, 'gay porn' will always refer to gay *male* porn.
2 For a general introduction to this, see Lesage (1981) and the bibliography in Marchetti (1981).

3 This access is not actually so easy outside of certain major metropolitan centres and recent police practices in Great Britain have hit gay porn far more decisively than straight.

4 'Because it is less specific, less suggestive of actual sexual activity, "erotica" is regularly used as a euphemism for "classy porn". Pornography expressed in literary language or expensive photography and consumed by the upper middle class is "erotica"; the cheap stuff, which can't pretend to any purpose but getting people off, is smut.' Ellen Willis, quoted in Carter (1981: 20–38).

5 An example of this is the role of the representation of the body in Christian iconography. At one level, the body of Christ could not be a more central motif of Christianity, most notably in the image of Christ on the cross. But the tendency remains to stress what the body means at the expense of what it is, to highlight transcendence over the body. In the Christian story of Christ as the Word made flesh, it is the Word that ultimately matters, not the flesh.

6 The magazine *m/f* is the leading example of this.

7 For a critique of idealism, Lovell (1980).

8 The one area of cultural work that has been concerned with body knowledge is dance, but the leading exponents of Modern Dance such as Isadora Duncan and Ruth St Denis have been influentially committed to notions of natural movement. See Kendall (1979).

9 I am conscious that because this article, in a manner of speaking, attacks things I have written – and even attacks what it infers from them about my sexual practices – I may here treat the article rather unfairly.

10 This is only one element of any full analysis. One of the major elements not discussed here, and that needs work doing on it, is the role of iconography – of dress and setting, and especially performers, the male types that are used, porn stars' images and so on, all drenched in ideological meanings.

11 For further discussion see Martin (1980).

12 For a discussion of this difficult nature/nurture debate from a socialist feminist perspective that does not discount the contribution of biology altogether, see Sayers (1982).

13 Waugh (1985) disputes the assertion in this paragraph.

14 This is a question of degree – producers and audiences are not equal in their power of determining the form that representation takes, and especially in a field so fiercely colonized by capitalist exploitation as pornography; and at the psychological level, performers and audience members are not necessarily equal, in that performers are validated as attractive sexual beings to a degree that audience members may not be. But the point is that they are all gay men participating in a gay sub-culture, a situation that does not hold with heterosexual porn. See Siebenand (1980) and Waugh (1985).

REFERENCES

Aitken, Will (1981–2) 'Erect in the dark', *Gay News* (Winter Extra December/January): 15–20.

Allen, Deborah and Harris, Gavin (1982) 'Languages of rage and revenge', *Gay Information* 9/10: 20–7.

Barrett, Michèle (1980) *Women's Oppression Today*, London: Verso.

Blachford, Gregg (1978) 'Looking at pornography', *Gay Left* 6: 16–20.

Carter, Mick (1981) 'The re-education of desire: some thoughts on current erotic visual practices', *Art and Text* 4: 20–38.

Dworkin, Andrea (1981) *Pornography: Men Possessing Women*, New York: Putnam's.

Ehrenstein, David (1980) 'Within the pleasure principle, or irresponsible homosexual propaganda', *Wide Angle* 4 (1): 62–5.

Faust, Beatrice (1982) *Women, Sex and Pornography*, Harmondsworth, Mx: Penguin.

Foucault, Michel (1980) *The History of Sexuality*, Vol. 1, trans. Robert Hurley, New York: Vintage.

Giles, Dennis (1976) 'Angel on fire', *Velvet Light Trap* 16.

Griffin, Susan (1981) *Pornography and Silence*, London: Women's Press.

Hocquenghem, Guy (1978) *Homosexual Desire*, London: Allison & Busby.

Kendall, Elizabeth (1979) *Where She Danced*, New York: Alfred Knopf.

Lederer, Laura (ed.) (1980) *Take Back the Night*, New York: William Morrow.

Lesage, Julia (1981) 'Women and pornography', *Jump Cut* 26: 46–7, 60.

Lovell, Terry (1980) *Pictures of Reality*, London: British Film Institute.

McDonald, Boyd (ed.) (1981) *Meat*, San Francisco, CA: Gay Sunshine Press.

Marchetti, Gina (1981) 'Readings on women and pornography', *Jump Cut* 26: 56–60.

Martin, Angela (1980) 'Chantal Akerman's films: a dossier', *Feminist Review* 3: 24–47.

Mele, Sam and Thirkell, Mark (1981) 'Pornographic narrative', *Gay Information* 6: 10–13.

Myers, Kathy (1982) 'Towards a feminist erotica', *Camerawork* 24: 14–16, 19.

Rich, B. Ruby (1982), review of the film *Not a Love Story*, *Village Voice*, 20 July.

Sayers, Janet (1982) *Biological Politics*, London: Tavistock.

Siebenand, Paul Alcuin (1980) *The Beginnings of Gay Cinema in Los Angeles: the Industry and the Audience*, Ann Arbor, Mich.: University of Michigan Press.

Waugh, Thomas (1985) 'Men's pornography: gay vs straight', *Jump Cut* 30: 30–6.

Wilson, Elizabeth (1983) *What Is To Be Done About Violence Against Women?* Harmondsworth, Middx: Penguin.
Winship, Janice (1982), review of Andrea Dworkin (1981) *Pornography: Men Possessing Women*, *Feminist Review* 11: 97–100.

FURTHER READING

Henderson, Lisa (1992) 'Lesbian pornography: cultural transgression and sexual demystification', in Sally Munt (ed.) *Being There: New Lesbian Criticism*, London: Harvester.
Patton, Cindy (1988) 'The cum shot: three takes on lesbian and gay sexuality', *Outlook* 1 (3): 72–7.
Ross, Andrew (1989) *No Respect: Intellectuals and Popular Culture*, New York and London: Routledge.
Watney, Simon (1987) *Policing Desire*, London: Comedia/Methuen.
Waugh, Thomas (1983) 'A heritage of pornography', *The Body Politic* 90: 29–33.
Williams, Linda (1990) *Hard Core: the Frenzy of the Visible*, Berkeley, CA: University of California Press.

12 It's being so camp as keeps us going

Arguments have lasted all night about what camp really is and what it means. There are two different interpretations which connect at certain points – camping about is one, mincing and screaming. The other is a certain taste in art and entertainment, a certain sensibility.

Camping about has a lot to be said for it. First of all and above all, it's very us. It is a distinctive way of behaving and of relating to each other that we have evolved. To have a good camp together gives you a tremendous sense of identification and belonging. It is just about the only style, language and culture that is distinctively and unambiguously gay male. One of our greatest problems I think is that we are cut adrift for most of the time in a world drenched in straightness. All the images and words of the society express and confirm the rightness of heterosexuality. Camp is one thing that expresses and confirms being a gay man.

Then again camp is fun. It's quite easy to pick up the lingo and get into the style, and it makes even quite dull people witty. Fun and wit are their own justification, but camp fun has other merits too. It's a form of self-defence. Particularly in the past, the fact that gay men could so sharply and brightly make fun of themselves meant that the real awfulness of their situation could be kept at bay – they need not take things too seriously, need not let it get them down. Camp kept, and keeps, a lot of gay men going.

And camp is not masculine. By definition, camping about is not butch. So camp is a way of being human, witty and vital (for the whole camp stance is full of vitality), without conforming to the drabness and rigidity of the hetero male role. You've only got to think of the impact of Quentin Crisp's high camp (accurately enough charted in the Thames TV film *The Naked Civil Servant*) on the straight world he came up against, to see that camp has a radical/progressive potential: scaring muggers who know that all this butch male bit is not really them but who feel they have to act as if it is (Quentin showed that he knew they were screamers underneath it all); running rings of logic and wit round the pedestrian ideas of psychiatrists, magistrates and the rest; and developing by living out a high camp life-style a serenity and a sense of being at-one-with-yourself (caught in the beautifully camp line, 'I am one of the stately homos of Britain').

Identity and togetherness, fun and wit, self-protection and thorns in the flesh of straight society – these are the pluses of camp. Unfortunately there are also minuses, and they are precisely the opposite side of those positive features.

The togetherness you get from camping about is fine – but not everybody actually feels able to camp about. A bunch of queens scream- ing together can be very exclusive for someone who isn't a queen or feels unable to camp. The very tight togetherness that makes it so good to be one of the queens is just the thing that makes a lot of other gay men feel left out. One of the sadder features of the gay movement is the down so many activists have on queens and camp – on the only heritage we've got. But it can work the other way around too – some queens despise the straight-looking (or otherwise non-queenly) gays around them, as if camping about is the only way of being gay. You have to let people be gay in the way that's best for them.

The fun, the wit, has its drawbacks too. It tends to lead to an attitude that you can't take anything seriously, everything has to be turned into a witticism or a joke. Camp finds CHE[1] too dull, GLF[2] too political, all the movement activities just not fun enough. It's a fair point, up to a point – CHE and GLF can be a bit glum and a bit heavy. But actually they've got quite a serious job to do. Life is not a bed of roses for gay men, still; sexism and our own male chauvinism are hard to understand, come to terms with, change. That does not always lend itself to fun and wit, but it needs to be done all the same.

Again, the self-mockery of self-protection can have a corrosive effect on us. We can keep mocking ourselves to the point where we really do think we're a rather pathetic, inferior lot. Phrases like 'silly Nelly', 'Chance 'd be a fine thing' and 'It's too much for a white woman', funny though they are, have a lot that is self-hating about them – behind them linger such ideas as 'How stupid I am', 'I'm too wretched and ugly to attract anyone', 'I'm too sexually hung-up to be able to give myself physically'. . . . Camp can help us from letting the social, cultural situation of gays getting us down: but it is the situation that's wrong, not ourselves. Camp sometimes stops us seeing that.

Camping about then is good and bad, progressive and reactionary. Often it's very hard to disentangle these two aspects. For instance, I am very much in the habit of calling men 'she': a man with a large cock is 'a big girl'; to a man showing off, I'll say 'Get her!'; I welcome friends with 'It's Miss Jones' (or whatever the man's name is). In one way, this is a good habit. After all, I'm glad to be gay and I prefer straight women (i.e. most women) to straight men (i.e. most men). Calling gay men 'she' means I don't think of them, or myself, as straight men (with all that that implies). But given the actual situation of women in society, and given that however hard I try, there's still plenty of male chauvinism about me, there is something rather suspect about this habit. Isn't it tantamount to saying gay men are inferior to straight men, just as women are? Isn't it really a put-down of gay men, and of women? It's hard to decide, and in the end I think I'll go on doing it because I'd rather gay men identified with straight women than with straight men, since most of the values associated with masculinity in this society (aggressiveness, competitiveness, being 'above' tenderness and emotion) I reject. Yet the whole practice, like so much of camp, is deeply ambiguous. So much depends on what you feel about men and women, about sex, about being gay.

The context of camp is important too. Camp means a lot at a gathering of gay people, or used defiantly by open gays against straightness: but it is very easily taken up by straight society and used against us. We know two things about camp that straights, at any rate as the media and everyday jokes show it, don't – that it is nice to be a queen (can be, should be); and that not all gay men are queens. The straight media have taken up the queen image which we have created but use it against us. To a limited extent, they appreciate the wit, but they don't see why it was necessary. They pick up the undertow of self-oppression without ever latching on to the elements of criticism and defiance of straightness. And they just never seem to realize that camping is only one way of being gay. Camp queens are the inevitable image of gayness in art and the media. As I see it, this rather catches us in a cleft stick. We should defend camp, whether we're queens or not; at the same time, we've got to make it clear that we are not all camp all the same. That's a rather complicated argument for the straight media. It's also quite a complicated problem for us too – but ultimately I think we should be open about allowing each other to be queens or not as we feel, and should try to build on the anti-butch fun and wit legacy of camp as a way of building gayness into a better society.

What then of camp as a kind of taste or sensibility?

It is easy, and usual, to offer a list of camp things at the beginning of discussions of camp, so that we all know what we are talking about. Thus:

Nelson Eddy and Jeanette MacDonald
Aubrey Beardsley
Vienna waltzes
most classical ballet
Busby Berkeley
the Queen Mother

Ronald Firbank
velvet and brocade curtains
Marlene Dietrich.

Such lists are, however, a bit misleading, since camp is far more a question of how you respond to things rather than qualities actually inherent in those things. It's perfectly possible to take MacDonald and Eddy seriously as lovers in musicals, or the Queen Mother as an embodiment of Britannic royalty, or Beardsley as a draughtsman, and so on. Equally, you can find things camp which are, on the face of it, the very antithesis of camp – John Wayne, for instance, or Wagner. It's all a question of how you look at it.

How then to define the camp way of looking at things? Basically, it is a way of prising the form of something away from its content, of revelling in the style while dismissing the content as trivial. If you really believed in the emotions and stories of classical ballet, in the rightness and value of royalty, in the properness of supervirility and fascism, then you could not find *The Sleeping Beauty*, the Queen Mother, or John Wayne camp. What I value about camp is that it is precisely a weapon against the mystique surrounding art, royalty and masculinity – it cocks an irresistible snook, it demystifies by playing up the artifice by means of which such things as these retain their hold on the majority of the population.

It is interesting to speculate about why it is that camp should be the form that male gay culture has taken. Susan Sontag, in a marvellous essay on camp in her book *Against Interpretation*, suggests that camp is the way gay men have sought to make some impression on the culture of the society they live in. Mastery of style and wit has been a way of declaiming that gays have something distinctive to offer society. This seems to me to be true. Gay men have made certain 'style professions' very much theirs (at any rate by association, even if not necessarily in terms of the numbers of gays actually employed in these professions) – hairdressing, interior decoration, dress design, ballet, musicals, revue. These occupations have made the life of society as a whole more elegant and graceful, and the show-biz end has provided the world at large with many pleasant evenings. At the same time hairdressing, interior decoration and the rest are clearly marked with the camp sensibility – they are style for style's sake, they don't have 'serious' content (a hairstyle is not 'about' anything), they don't have a practical use (they're just nice), and the actual forms taken accentuate artifice, fun and occasionally outrageousness – all that chi-chi and tat, those pinks and lace and sequins and tassels, curlicues and 'features' in the hair, satin drapes and chiffon scarves and fussy ornaments, all the paraphernalia of a camp sensibility that has provided gay men with a certain legitimacy in the world.

A certain legitimacy only. The very luxuriousness and 'uselessness' of

Figure 12.1 The Queen Mother

Figure 12.2 Marlene Dietrich

Figure 12.3 Jeanette MacDonald and Nelson Eddy

Figure 12.4 John Wayne

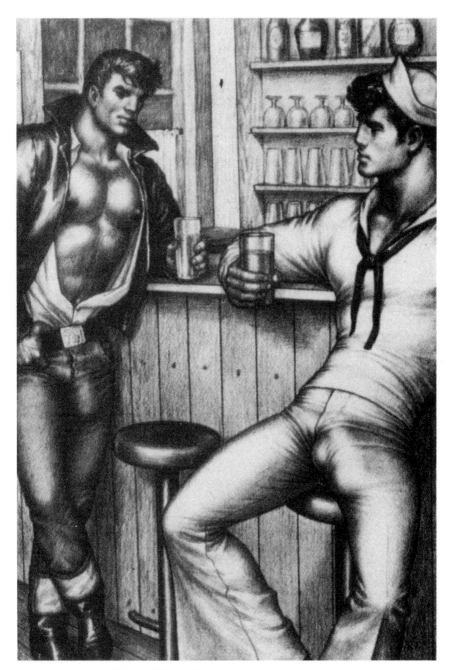

Figure 12.5 Two of Tom of Finland's men

these professions have also tended to reinforce the image of gay men as decadent, marginal, frivolous – above all, not involved in the real production of wealth (on the shopfloor or in the management offices) in society, just sterile parasites on the edges. And too the association of so much of the camp style professions with women is ambiguous. Although women in our society are involved in production, none the less their social role is seen as being adjuncts to men, not just to provide a man with a wife, servant and mother to 'his' kids, but also to display his wealth by her smartness, the frequency of her hair-dos, the number of her frocks. This applies above all to the wealthy of course, where the lady in her Paris fashions displays her husband's buying power and her access (by virtue of his position) to the canons of fashion and good taste. But in less spectacular forms it works further down the social scale. Most husbands expect their wives to 'look nice', to make an effort with their appearance when they take them out. It is only the poorest husband whose wife cannot afford a bouffant hair-do, some fake fur and a glass brooch for Saturday night out. And we gay men, have been deeply involved in creating the styles and providing the services for the 'turn-out' of the women of the western world. This gives us legitimacy – but as parasites on women, who are themselves seen as subordinate to men and objects of luxury (however meagre). Moreover, the involvement of camp in objectifying women in this way (reaching its apotheosis in Busby Berkeley's production numbers – though I've never heard that he himself was gay) makes it something that anyone who cares about everyone's liberation should be wary of.

But that's a digression. Let's get back to the point about camp evolving because gay men have staked out a claim on society at large by mastery of style and artifice. That seems true, but the question still remains: why style and artifice rather than anything else? A reason is suggested by a German survey of gay people, the results of which were published in an early *Gay News* (London). They found that gays were extremely 'adaptable'; that is, we tend to find it easy to fit in to any occupation, or set-up, or circle of people. Or rather, and this is the point, we find it easy to appear to fit in, we are good at picking up the rules, conventions, forms and appearances of different social circles. And why? Because we've had to be good at it, we've had to be good at disguise, at appearing to be one of the crowd, the same as everyone else. Because we had to hide what we really felt (gayness) for so much of the time, we had to master the façade of whatever social set-up we found ourselves in – we couldn't afford to stand out in any way, for it might give the game away about our gayness. So we have developed an eye and an ear for surfaces, appearances, forms – style. Small wonder then that when we came to develop our own culture, the habit of style should have remained so dominant in it.

Looked at in this way, the camp sensibility is very much a product of our oppression. And, inevitably, it is scarred by that oppression. Some of the minuses of camp as a sensibility I've already mentioned – the relegation of its practitioners to licensed decorators on the edges of society, its involvement with the objectification of women. Other minuses resemble the drawbacks of camp behaviour.

The emphasis on surface and style can become obsessive – nothing can be taken seriously, anything deep or problematic or heavy is shimmied away from in a flurry of chic. Camp seems often unable to discriminate between those things that need to be treated for laughs and style, and those that are genuinely serious and important.

Besides this, camp is so beguiling that it has been adopted by many straights of late. (Think of the tone of much criticism of the arts these days – BBC2's *Film Night*, nostalgia books, the TV criticism of Clive James and Nancy Banks-Smith.) But something happens to camp when taken over by straights – it loses its cutting edge, its identification with the gay experience, its distance from the straight sexual world-view. Take the example of John Wayne. Many straight men find him camp now, but they love him just the same. Gay camp can emphasize what a production number the Wayne image is – the lumbering gait, drawling voice and ever more craggy face are a deliberately constructed and manufactured image of virility. In this way, gay camp can stop us from treating John Wayne as an embodiment of what it 'really' means to be a man. Straight camp puts a different emphasis. The authority, power and roughness of the Wayne image are still dear to the straight imagination, but they have been criticized heavily enough in recent years (by gays and camp among others) for there to be embarrassment about directly accepting or endorsing such qualities. Camp allows straight audiences to reject the style of John Wayne; but because it is so pleasant to laugh, it also allows for a certain wistful affection for him to linger on. However, affection for John Wayne can only be in reality affection for that way of being a man. Straight camp allows images of butchness to retain their hold even while they are apparently being rejected.

Of course, this twisting of camp away from its radical/progressive/ critical potential is only possible because of the ambiguity of camp even within gay circles. (For instance, the drawings of Tom of Finland are at one level over-the-top camp, but also clearly a turn-on too.) Not all gay camp is in fact progressive, but none the less it does have the potential of being so. What camp can do is to demystify the images and world-view of art and the media. We are encouraged by schooling to be very solemn in the presence of art; and we are tempted by film and television to be drawn into the worlds they present as if they were real. Camp can make us see that what art and the media give us are not the Truth or Reality but fabrications, particular ways of talking about the world, particular understandings and feelings of the way life is. Art and the media don't give us life as it really is – how could they ever? – but only life as artists and producers think it is. Camp, by drawing attention to the artifices employed by artists, can constantly remind us that what we are seeing is only a view of life. This doesn't stop us enjoying it, but it does stop us believing what we are shown too readily. It stops us thinking that those who create the landscape of culture know more about life than we do ourselves. A camp appreciation of art and the media can keep us on our guard against them – and considering their view of gayness, and sexuality in general, that's got to be a good thing.

In his introduction to the first *Playguy*[3] he edited, Roger Baker quoted Dennis Altman's lovely phrase, 'Camp is to gay what soul is to black'. That's right – but push at the resemblance a bit and you get to the ambiguities of both camp and soul. Soul is not unequivocally a good thing. Certainly, it provides blacks (some blacks) with a definitely black culture; with its roots in religion, it provides an openness to irrational experience that white culture tends to play down; and with its connections to dance and ritual, it allows for a physical freedom, a being-at-home-in-your-body, that repressed white culture shies away from. But soul also reinforces notions of black people as mindless, superstitious and sex-obsessed – it may at times hold them back from making claims on the equally human and useful attributes of rationality and restraint. There is the same equivocality about camp – it does give us (some of us) an identity, it does undercut sex roles and the dominant world-view, it is fun; but it can also trap us if we are not careful in the endless pursuit of enjoyment at any price, in a rejection of seriousness and depth of feeling. What we've got to do is to activate the positive attributes of camp – mince in the streets, send up Kojak and Burt Reynolds and Colt models, come together for a camp, keep our oppression at bay with a scream and a joke – without letting them trap us.

You know those clenched fists you get on political badges (including women's liberation and GLF)? Well, why shouldn't it be a clenched fist on a limp wrist? Divine.

NOTES

This chapter was originally published in 1976 in *Playguy* and was reprinted in 1977 in *The Body Politic* 36.

1 The Campaign for Homosexual Equality.
2 The Gay Liberation Front.
3 The British gay magazine which originally commissioned this article.

FURTHER READING

Babuscio, Jack (1977) 'Camp and the gay sensibility', in Richard Dyer (ed.) *Gays and Film*, London: British Film Institute, 40–57.

Boone, Bruce (1979) 'Gay language as political praxis: the poetry of Frank O'Hara', *Social Text* 1: 59–92.

Britton, Andrew (1978/9) 'FOR interpretation – notes against camp', *Gay Left* 7: 11–14.

Finch, Mark (1986) 'Sex and address in *Dynasty*', *Screen* 27 (6): 24–43.

Medhurst, Andy (1990) 'Pitching camp', *City Limits* (May 10–17): 18–19.

Russo, Vito (1979) 'Camp', in Martin P. Levene (ed.) *Gay Men: The Sociology of Male Homosexuality*, New York: Harper & Row, 205–10.

Sontag, Susan (1967) 'Notes on camp', in *Against Interpretation*, London: Eyre and Spottiswoode, 275–92.

13 In defence of disco

All my life I've liked the wrong music. I never liked Elvis and rock 'n' roll; I always preferred Rosemary Clooney. And since I became a socialist, I've often felt virtually terrorized by the prestige of rock and folk on the left. How could I admit to two Petula Clark LPs in the face of miners' songs from the north-east and the Rolling Stones? I recovered my nerve partially when I came to see show-biz-type music as a key part of gay culture, which, whatever its limitations, was a culture to defend. And I thought I'd really made it when I turned on to Tamla Motown, sweet soul sounds, disco. Chartbusters already, and I like them! Yet the prestige of folk and rock, and now punk and (rather patronizingly, I think) reggae, still holds sway. It's not just that people whose politics I broadly share don't *like* disco, they manage to imply that it is politically beyond the pale to like it. It's against this attitude that I want to defend disco (which otherwise, of course, hardly needs any defence).

I'm going to talk mainly about disco *music*, but there are two preliminary points I'd like to make. The first is that disco is more than just a form of music, although certainly the music is at the heart of it. Disco is also kinds of dancing, club, fashion, film, etc., in a word, a certain *sensibility*, manifest in music, clubs, etc., historically and culturally specific, economically, technologically, ideologically and aesthetically determined – and worth thinking about. Secondly, as a sensibility in music it encompasses more than what we would perhaps strictly call disco music, to include a lot of soul, Tamla and even the later work of 'Easy Listening' artistes like Peggy Lee and Johnny Mathis.

My defence is in two parts. First, a discussion of the arguments against disco in terms of its being 'capitalist' music. Second, an attempt to think through the – ambivalently, ambiguously, contradictorily – positive qualities of disco.

DISCO AND CAPITAL

Much of the hostility to disco stems from the equation of it with capitalism. Both in how it is produced and in what it expresses, disco is held to be irredeemably capitalistic.

Now it is unambiguously the case that disco is produced by capitalist industry, and since capitalism is an irrational and inhuman mode of production, the disco industry is as bad as all the rest. Of course. However, this argument has assumptions behind it that are more problematic. These are of two kinds. One assumption concerns *music as a mode of production*, and has to do with the belief that it is possible in a capitalist society to produce things (e.g. music, e.g. rock and folk) that are outside of the capitalist mode of production. Yet quite apart from the general point that such a position seeks to elevate activity outside of existing structures rather than struggles against them, the two kinds of music most often set against disco as a mode of production are not really convincing.

One is folk music – in Britain, people might point to Gaelic songs and industrial ballads – the kind of music often used, or reworked, in left fringe theatre. These, it is argued, are not, like disco (and pop music in general), produced for the people but by them. They are 'authentic' people's music. So they are – or rather, were. The problem is that we don't live in a society of small, technologically simple communities such as produce such art. Preserving such music at best gives us an historical perspective on peasant and working-class struggle, at worst leads to a nostalgia for a simple, harmonious community existence that never really existed. More bluntly, songs in Gaelic or dealing with nineteenth-century factory conditions, beautiful as they are, don't mean much to most English-speaking people today.

The other kind of music most often posed against disco and 'pap pop' at the level of how it is produced is rock (including Dylan-type folk and everything from early rock 'n' roll to progressive concept albums). The argument here is that rock is easily produced by non-professionals – all that is needed are a few instruments and somewhere to play – whereas disco music requires the whole panoply of recording studio technology, which makes it impossible for non-professionals (the kid in the streets) to produce. The factual accuracy of this observation needs supplementing with some other observations. Quite apart from the very rapid – but then bemoaned by some purists – move of rock into elaborate recording studios, even when it is simple, produceable by non-professionals, the fact is that rock is still quite expensive, and remains in practice largely the preserve of middle-class people who can afford electric guitars, music lessons, etc. (You have only to look at the biographies of those now professional rock musicians who started out in a simple non-professional way – the preponderance of public school and university educated young men in the field is rivalled only by their preponderance in the Labour Party front bench.) More importantly, this kind of music production is wrongly (except perhaps at certain key historical moments) thought of as being generated from the grass roots – non-professional music-making, in rock as elsewhere, bases itself, inevitably, on professional music. Any notion that rock emanates from 'the people' is soon confounded by the recognition that what 'the people' are doing is trying to be as much like professionals as possible.

The second kind of argument based on the fact that disco is produced by capitalism concerns *music as an ideological expression*. Here it is assumed that capitalism as a mode of production necessarily and simply produces 'capitalist' ideology. The theory of the relation between the mode of production and the ideologies of a particular society is too complicated and unresolved to be gone into here, but we can begin by remembering that capitalism is about profit. In the language of classical economics, capitalism produces commodities, and its interest in commodities is their exchange-value (how much profit they can realize) rather than their use-value (their social or human worth). This becomes particularly problematic for capitalism when dealing with an expressive commodity – such as disco – since a major problem for capitalism is that there is no necessary or guaranteed connection between exchange-value and use-value – in other words, capitalism as productive relations can just as well make a profit from something that is ideologically opposed to bourgeois society as something that supports it. As long as a commodity makes a profit, what does it matter? (I should like to acknowledge my debt to Terry Lovell for explaining this aspect of capitalist cultural production to me.) Indeed, it is because of this dangerous, anarchic tendency of capitalism that ideological institutions – the Church, the state, education, the family, etc. – are necessary. It is their job to make sure that what capitalism produces is in capitalism's longer-term interests. However, since they often don't know that that is their job, they don't always perform it. Cultural production within capitalist society is then founded on two profound contradictions: the first, between production for profit and production for use; the second, within those institutions whose job it is to regulate the first contradiction. What all this boils down to, in terms of disco, is that the fact that disco is produced by capitalism does not mean that it is automatically, necessarily, simply supportive of capitalism. Capitalism constructs the disco experience, but it does not necessarily know what it is doing, apart from making money.

I am not now about to launch into a defence of disco music as some great subversive art form. What the arguments above lead me to is, first, a basic point of departure in the recognition that cultural production under capitalism is necessarily contradictory, and, second, that it may well be the case that capitalist cultural products are most likely to be contradictory at just those points – such as disco – where they are most commercial and professional, where the urge to profit is at its strongest. Third, this mode of cultural production has produced a commodity, disco, that has been taken up by gays in ways that may well not have been intended by its producers. The anarchy of capitalism throws up commodities that an oppressed group can take up and use to cobble together its own culture. In this respect, disco is very much like another profoundly ambiguous aspect of male gay culture, camp. It is a 'contrary' use of what the dominant culture provides, it is important in forming a gay identity, and it has subversive potential as well as reactionary implications.

THE CHARACTERISTICS OF DISCO

Let me turn now to what I consider to be the three important characteristics of disco – eroticism, romanticism and materialism. I'm going to talk about them in terms of what it seems to me they mean within the context of gay culture. These three characteristics are not in themselves good or bad (any more than disco music as a whole is), and they need specifying more precisely. What is interesting is how they take us to qualities that are not only key ambiguities within gay male culture, but have also traditionally proved stumbling blocks to socialists.

Eroticism

It can be argued that all popular music is erotic. What we need to define is the specific way of thinking and feeling erotically in disco. I'd like to call it 'whole body' eroticism, and to define it by comparing it with the eroticism of the two kinds of music to which disco is closest – popular song (i.e. the Gershwin, Cole Porter, Burt Bacharach type of song) and rock.

Popular song's eroticism is 'disembodied': it succeeds in expressing a sense of the erotic which yet denies eroticism's physicality. This can be shown by the nature of tunes in popular songs and the way they are handled.

Popular song's tunes are rounded off, closed, self-contained. They achieve this by adopting a strict musical structure (AABA) in which the opening melodic phrases are returned to and, most importantly, the tonic note of the whole song is also the last note of the tune. (The tonic note is the note that forms the basis for the key in which the song is written; it is therefore the harmonic 'anchor' of the tune and closing on it gives precisely a feeling of 'anchoring', coming to a settled stop.) Thus although popular songs often depart – especially in the middle section (B) – from their melodic and harmonic beginnings, they also always return to them. This gives them – even at their most passionate, say, Porter's 'Night and Day' – a sense of security and containment. The tune is not allowed to invade the whole of one's body. Compare the typical disco tune, which is often little more than an endlessly repeated phrase which drives beyond itself, is not 'closed off'. Even when disco music uses a popular song standard, it often turns it into a simple phrase. Gloria Gaynor's version of Porter's 'I've Got You Under My Skin', for instance, is in large part a chanted repetition of 'I've got you'.

Popular song's lyrics place its tunes within a conceptualization of love and passion as emanating from 'inside', the heart or the soul. Thus the yearning cadences of popular song express an erotic yearning of the inner person, not the body. Once again, disco refuses this. Not only are the lyrics often more directly physical and the delivery more raunchy (e.g. Grace Jones's 'I Need a Man'), but, most importantly, disco is insistently rhythmic in a way that popular song is not.

Rhythm, in western music, is traditionally felt as being more physical than other musical elements such as melody, harmony and instrumentation. This is why western music is traditionally so dull rhythmically – nothing expresses our Puritan heritage more vividly. It is to other cultures that we have had to turn – and above all to Afro-American culture – to learn about rhythm. The history of popular song since the late nineteenth century is largely the history of the white incorporation (or ripping off) of black music – ragtime, the Charleston, the tango, swing, rock'n'roll, rock. Now what is interesting about this incorporation/ripping-off is what it meant and means. Typically, black music was thought of by the white culture as being both more primitive and more 'authentically' erotic. Infusions of black music were always seen as (and often condemned as) sexual and physical. The use of insistent black rhythms in disco music, recognizable by the closeness of the style to soul and reinforced by such characteristic features of black music as the repeated chanted phrase and the use of various African percussion instruments, means that it inescapably signifies (in this white context) physicality.

However, rock is as influenced by black music as disco is. This then leads me to the second area of comparison between disco's eroticism and rock's. The difference between them lies in what each 'hears' in black music. Rock's eroticism is thrusting, grinding – it is not whole body, but phallic. Hence it takes from black music the insistent beat and makes it even more driving; rock's repeated phrases trap you in their relentless push, rather than releasing you in an open-ended succession of repetitions as disco does. Most revealing perhaps is rock's instrumentation. Black music has more percussion instruments than white, but it knows how to use them to create all sorts of effect – light, soft, lively, as well as heavy, hard and grinding. Rock, however, only hears the latter and develops the percussive qualities of essentially non-percussive instruments to increase this, hence the twanging electric guitar and the nasal vocal delivery. One can see how, when rock'n'roll first came in, this must have been a tremendous liberation from popular song's disembodied eroticism – here was a really physical music, and not just mealy-mouthedly physical, but quite clear what it was about – cock. But rock confines sexuality to cock (and this is why, no matter how progressive the lyrics and even when performed by women, rock remains indelibly phallocentric music). Disco music, on the other hand, hears the physicality in black music and its range. It achieves this by a number of features including: the sheer amount going on rhythmically in even quite simple disco music (for rhythmic clarity with complexity, listen to the full-length version of the Temptations' 'Papa was a Rolling Stone'); the willingness to play with rhythm, delaying it, jumping it, countering it rather than simply driving on and on (examples: Patti Labelle, Isaac Hayes); the range of percussion instruments used and with different affects (e.g. the spiky violins in Quincy Jones/Herbie Hancock's 'Tell Me a Bedtime Story': the gentle pulsations of George Benson). This never stops being erotic, but it restores eroticism to the whole of the body, and for both sexes, not just confining it to the penis. It leads to the expressive, sinuous movement of disco dancing, not just that mixture of awkwardness and thrust so dismally characteristic of dancing to rock.

Gay men do not intrinsically have any prerogative over whole body eroticism. We are often even more cock-oriented than non-gays of either sex, and it depresses me that such phallic forms of disco as Village People should be so gay identified. None the less, partly because many of us have traditionally not thought of ourselves as being 'real men' and partly because gay ghetto culture is also a space where alternative definitions, including of sexuality, can be developed, it seems to me that the importance of disco in scene culture indicates an openness to a sexuality that is not defined in terms of cock. Although one cannot easily move from musical values to personal ones, or from personal ones to politically effective ones, it is at any rate suggestive that gay culture should promote a form of music that denies the centrality of the phallus while at the same time refusing the non-physicality which such a denial has hitherto implied.

Romanticism

Not all disco music is romantic. The lyrics of many disco hits are either straightforward sexual – not to say sexist – or else broadly social (e.g. Detroit Spinners' 'Ghetto Child', Stevie Wonder's 'Living in the City'), and the hard drive of Village People or Labelle is positively anti-romantic. Yet there is none the less a strong strain of romanticism in disco. This can be seen in the lyrics, which often differ little from popular song standards, and indeed often are standards (e.g. 'What a Difference a Day Made' – Esther Phillips, 'La Vie en Rose' – Grace

Jones). More impressively, it is the instrumentation and arrangements of disco music that are so romantic.

The use of massed violins takes us straight back, via Hollywood, to Tchaikovsky, to surging, outpouring emotions. A brilliant example is Gloria Gaynor's 'I've Got You Under My Skin', where in the middle section the violins take a hint from one of Porter's melodic phrases and develop it away from his tune in an ecstatic, soaring movement. This 'escape' from the confines of popular song into ecstacy is very character-istic of disco music, and nowhere more consistently than in such Diana Ross classics as 'Reach Out' and 'Ain't No Mountain High Enough'. This latter, with its lyrics' total surrender to love, its heavenly choir and sweeping violins, is perhaps one of the most extravagant reaches of disco's romanticism. But Ross is also a key figure in the gay appropria-tion of disco.

What Ross's records do – and I'm thinking basically of her work up to *Greatest Hits* volume 1 and the *Touch Me in the Morning* album – is express the intensity of fleeting emotional contacts. They are all-out expressions of adoration which yet have built in to them the recognition of the (inevitably) temporary quality of the experience. This can be a straight-forward lament for having been let down by a man, but more often it is both a celebration of a relationship and the almost willing recognition of its passing and the exquisite pain of its passing:

Remember me
As a sunny day
That you once had
Along the way . . .

If I've got to be strong
Don't you know I need to have tonight when you're gone
When you go I'll lie here
And think about
The last time that you
Touch me in the morning.

This last number, with Ross's 'unreally' sweet, porcelain, fragile voice and the string backing, concentrates that sense of celebrating the inten-sity of the passing relationship that haunts so much of her work. No wonder Ross is (was?) so important in gay male scene culture, for she both reflects what that culture takes to be an inevitable reality (that relationships don't last) and at the same time celebrates it, validates it.

Not all disco music works in this vein, yet in both some of the more sweetly melancholy orchestrations (even of lively numbers, like 'You Should Be Dancing' in *Saturday Night Fever*) and some of the lyrics and general tone (e.g. Donna Summer's *Four Seasons of Love* album), there is a carry-over of this emotional timbre. At a minimum then, disco's romanticism provides an embodiment and validation of an aspect of gay culture.

But romanticism is a particularly paradoxical quality of art to come to terms with. Its passion and intensity embody or create an experience that negates the dreariness of the mundane and everyday. It gives us a glimpse of what it means to live at the height of our emotional and experiental capacities – not dragged down by the banality of organized routine life. Given that everyday banality, work, domesticity, ordinary sexism and racism, are rooted in the structures of class and gender of this society, the flight from that banality can be seen as – is – a flight from capitalism and patriarchy themselves as lived experiences.

What makes this more complicated is the actual situation within which disco occurs. Disco is part of the wider to-and-fro between work and leisure, alienation and escape, boredom and enjoyment that we are so accustomed to (and which *Saturday Night Fever* plugs into so effectively). Now this to-and-fro is partly the mechanism by which we keep going, at work, at home – the respite of leisure gives us the energy for work, and anyway we are still largely brought up to think of leisure as a 'reward' for work. The circle locks us into it. But what happens in that space of leisure can be profoundly significant – it is there that we may learn about an alternative to work and to society as it is. Romanticism is one of the major modes of leisure in which this sense of an alternative is kept alive. Romanticism asserts that the limits of work and domesticity are not the limits of experience.

I don't say that the passion and intensity of romanticism is a political ideal we could strive for – I doubt that it is humanly possible to live permanently at that pitch. What I do believe is that the movement between banality and something 'other' than banality is an essential dialectic of society, a constant keeping open of a gap between what is and what could or should be. Herbert Marcuse in the currently unfashionable *One-Dimensional Man* argues that our society tries to close that gap, to assert that what is is all that there could be, is what should be. For all its commercialism and containment within the work:leisure to-and-fro, I think disco romanticism is one of the things that can keep the gap open, that can allow the *experience of contradiction* to continue. Since I also believe that political struggle is rooted in experience (though utterly doomed if left at it), I find this dimension of disco potentially positive. (A further romantic/utopian aspect of disco is realized in the non-commercial discos organized by gay and women's groups. Here a moment of community can be achieved, often in circle dances or simply in the sense of knowing people as people, not anonymous bodies. Fashion is less important, and sociability correspondingly more so. This can be achieved in smaller clubs, perhaps especially outside the centre of London, which, when not just grotty monuments to self-oppression, can function as supportive expressions of something like a gay community.)

Materialism

Disco is characteristic of advanced capitalist societies simply in terms of the scale of money squandered on it. It is a riot of consumerism, dazzling in its technology (echo chambers, double and more tracking, electric instruments), overwhelming in its scale (banks of violins, massed choirs, the limitless range of percussion instruments), lavishly gaudy in the mirrors and tat of discothèques, the glitter and denim flash of its costumes. Its tacky sumptuousness is well evoked in the film *Thank God It's Friday*. Gone are the restraint of popular song, the sparseness of rock and reggae, the simplicity of folk. How can a socialist, or someone trying to be a feminist, defend it?

In certain respects, it is doubtless not defensible. Yet socialism and feminism are both forms of materialism – why is disco, a celebration of materiality if ever there was one, not therefore the appropriate art form of materialist politics?

Partly, obviously, because materialism in politics is not to be confused with mere matter. Materialism seeks to understand how things are in terms of how they have been produced and constructed in history, and how they can be better produced and constructed. This certainly does not mean immersing oneself in the material world – indeed, it includes deliberately stepping back from the material world to see what makes it the way it is and how to change it. Yes, but, materialism is also based on the profound conviction that politics is about the material world, and indeed that human life and the material world are all there is, no God, no magic forces. One of the dangers of materialist politics is that it is in constant danger of spiritualizing itself, partly because of the historical legacy of the religious forms that brought materialism into existence, partly because materialists have to work so hard not to take matter at face value that they often end up not treating it as matter at all. Disco's celebration of materiality is only a celebration of the world we are necessarily and always immersed in, and disco's materiality, in its technological modernity, is resolutely historical and cultural – it can never be, as most art claims for itself, an 'emanation' outside of history and of human production.

Disco's combination of romanticism and materialism effectively tells us – lets us experience – that we live in a world of materiality, that we can enjoy materiality but that the experience of materiality is not necessarily what the everyday world assures us it is. Its eroticism allows us to rediscover our bodies as part of this experience of materiality and the possibility of change.

If this sounds over the top, let one thing be clear – disco can't change the world, make the revolution. No art can do that, and it is pointless expecting it to. But partly by opening up experience, partly by changing definitions, art, disco, can be used. To which one might risk adding the refrain – If it feels good, *use* it.

NOTE

This chapter was originally published in 1979 in *Gay Left* 8.

FURTHER READING

Frith, Simon (1981) *Sound Effects*, London: Constable.
Savage, Jon (1990) 'Tainted love: the influence of male homosexuality and sexual divergence on pop music and culture since the war', in Alan Tomlinson (ed.) *Consumption, Identity and Style*, London: Routledge.

14 Getting over the rainbow: identity and pleasure in gay cultural politics

The 1970s saw the growth of many forms of cultural politics. Not since the years immediately following the Russian Revolution have socialists been so heavily and actively aware of the importance of cultural politics. The gay movement has had a special role to play here, above all in showing how a politics of culture can be rooted in, and grow out of, the already existing culture of an oppressed group. The gay movement activated the political potential of what lesbians and gay men had already achieved in developing against the grain of oppression: a particular way of life, a culture. I want to argue that this relation between a movement and the lived culture of the group that it represents can serve as an object lesson for the left. In addition, I suggest that the particular concerns of identity and pleasure, brought to political flower from the ground of the gay sub-culture, indicate specific ways of connecting political aims with the way people actually think and feel about their lives.

The development of gay culture is a classic instance of Marx's dictum that 'people make their own history, but they do not make it just as they please; they do not make it under circumstances chosen by themselves, but under circumstances directly encountered, given and transmitted from the past' (Marx 1977: 96). This is a dictum that all branches of the left need to integrate into their thinking and their political agenda.

The case of lesbians and gay men is exemplary but also extreme, in the sense that culture *is* the situation of gay people. Gays are defined and structurally placed in the sphere of culture – there are the circumstances that are not of our own choosing. Having been so placed, gays have sought to gain control over those conditions and in the process have produced a wealth of new cultural forms, new definitions of identity, new awarenesses of human happiness.

To understand this further, we need to consider first the question of the very concept 'homosexual', before going on to the issue of why culture is so privileged an arena of gay movement activity and the significance of some of the forms it takes. It is wrong to think of homosexuality – or almost any aspect of human body activity – as a biological given. Rather, we need to consider how 'the homosexual' has emerged historically as a *social construct*: an idea, and also a way of placing people socially, which has only come about in the last two centuries. There are two main points to stress when making this argument.

First, it is clear that bodily (including genital) contact between persons of the same sex is indeed universal. However, just as with bodily contact between persons of the opposite sex, same sex contact never exists outside a particular social formation. No body contact ever occurs in a social vacuum, and hence is never experienced in a purely 'biological' way. Thus although same sex body contact occurs throughout all history (and incidentally in the animal kingdom) it is never in any given instance ahistorical. What is remarkable about developments since the eighteenth century is the way that body activity has been narrowed down to be also the designation of a certain sort of person. Where once same sex body contact might be recognized as an activity (albeit, in our society, sinful) that people might be involved in, now there is a term, 'the homosexual', for persons who are socially/clinically defined as those who habitually involve themselves in same sex contact. 'Homosexual', a nineteenth-century coinage, designates persons not acts.

Part of the reason for using the laborious mouthful 'same sex body contact' is now I hope evident. It is a problem to use the word 'homosexual' outside the historical period of the word's currency, for we risk blurring the very point that needs to be made, namely that 'homosexuality', as our society calls it and understands it, did not exist outside the actual existence of the word. There is a further reason for avoiding the term – and indeed, now, politically, shunning it – and that is that it focuses so exclusively on the element of genital contact. This leads us to the second stage of the argument about the concept of the homosexual.

The word 'sexual' is notoriously hard to handle, since what one person finds sexual another does not. However, in general usage, the word does imply some degree of genital arousal and activity. There is no reason why we should not have a word that focuses on one particular body organ, but the word, and the history that surrounds it, has the effect of privileging genital functions over all others. Thus bodily relations between persons of the same sex, once they are designated 'homosexual', come to be seen entirely in terms of genitality. This is so even when actual genital activity is felt not to have taken place, as in the common supposed defence of homosexuals (and especially lesbians) that 'it's all right, they don't *do* anything'. This is a doubly offensive, and symptomatic, lie, since it both assumes genital activity would be wrong and at the same time implies that 'doing' and 'screwing' are synonymous, as if the limit of body relations between the same sex is genital. The power of ideas of sexuality is quite extraordinary, for not only do they focus attention on the genitals to the exclusion of all else, but they also have a tendency to reduce other aspects of human life to genital activity. This permeates common-sense thought. How often in conversation are a person's motives construed in terms of sexual desire, how often people's problems assumed to be sexual at root. It has become a habit in western society to look to sexuality as the explain-all of life, to see the fulfilment and frustration of genital desire as the key to the truth about what people want in general, what they do and what they are.

That 'the homosexual' is a modern social category, and that sexuality is a word with attendant institutional and social support that privileges the genitals in our understanding of the human body and its relation to being human: these two ideas inform most of what follows. One point must be made clear. The fact that 'the homosexual' and 'sexuality' have just been discussed as ideas does not mean that they exist in a realm of pure spirit. They are ideas by which we live. They are the very means by which we know our place in society and experience our bodies. I live my life in those terms, though in constant struggle within and against them. I do think of myself as a homosexual or, on better days, as gay, and I feel defined as a person by those sexual designations and observe that that is how I am treated too. And I habitually over-privilege genital response and often conflate it with sensual, sensuous and emotional response. What I have just written is a personal way of stating the kinds of issue that I now wish to sketch out about gay cultural politics.

THE CENTRALITY OF CULTURE

Before looking at possible reasons why culture is so central to the gay movement, it would be as well to say something briefly about what I mean the terms 'culture' and 'gay culture' to refer to. I am using 'culture' in the very widest sense to refer not only to the arts but to all those products and practices that both express and constitute the forms, values and emotional structures of social life. The specific references I shall be making to gay culture will hardly touch 'the arts' at all, but will discuss, for reasons that will be spelt out later, dress, dancing, forms of relating in public and ways of using and relating to the human body. These are particular instances of the various and manifold forms and activities that constitute gay ways of making sense of the world.

It is important to stress that gay culture does not necessarily know itself as political, much less as politically progressive or socialist. But we cannot afford, anywhere on the left, to be dismissive of the way life is felt, thought and lived by both the people we represent and ourselves. It is within culture that homosexual identities and pleasures are formed. When I use the term 'gay culture', I mean to indicate *any* cultural practice that may be considered significantly homosexual, whether or not it is a radical practice. The term 'gay cultural politics' I restrict to cultural work within the gay movement itself or markedly informed by its perspectives. Again, such activity may well not be radical. It could also be purely reformist or else more centred on individualistic 'revolt' or on the creation of alternative life-styles *within* society as it is.

Reasons why culture is central to the gay movement can be approached through slightly different notions of what the word 'culture' means. First, culture can be used to refer to the ways in which a society thinks and feels about itself. It is the ensemble of ideas, representations and forms that are available to people in a society to make sense of themselves and their society. Culture is not innocent. It is grounded in the interests of the people who produce it and in this sense it is a very similar concept to that of ideology. Like ideology, culture does not operate in a unitary way within a society: it involves contradictions and often antagonisms both within and between social groupings – along lines of class, gender, race and such socially designated factors as sexual orientation. The advantage of the word 'culture' in the present context, rather than ideology, is that it insists on the *material* and *affective* dimension of making sense as well as on the *cognitive*.

Culture in this sense is where and how the very concept and definition of homosexuality are produced. Precisely because, as I have argued, homosexuality is not a biological given, any politics based upon or around it is already a politics of culture, a politics centred on the sense made of particular potentials of the body. Gay politics is always already cultural politics, whether we like it or not.

Second, the word 'culture' can also designate that sphere of life that is left over when the realm of necessity has been fulfilled. It is the realm of feelings, pleasure, reflection, leisure. It is of course entirely wrong to think that such things do not permeate every aspect of human existence, but a predominant and effective way of thinking about our lives puts necessity in one slot and culture in another. Necessity includes work to *produce* the maintenance of life, and the family and kinship to *reproduce* life. And by very definition gays are seen as being outside these.

But such struggles as the Gay Rights at Work Committee and the campaigns around lesbian mothers brilliantly disrupt the distinction between necessity and culture, between gays and productive/reproductive life. They demonstrate that gays are involved in the labour process and that gays do bear and bring up children. By insisting on gay rights at work, we insist that sexuality and emotion do not evaporate when we clock in but inform every aspect of life. By fighting for the rights of lesbians (and gay men) to the custody and care of children, we refuse the idea that heterosexual intercourse and a concern for life are the same thing.

Much of the 'public' panic surrounding such struggles derives from the way they blur the distinction between sexuality as a private, personal domain, and work and procreation as public and socially responsible. This panic serves to reinforce the idea that gays, by virtue of their sexuality, are to be defined as irrelevant to work and impossible as parents. *As gays* they are to be defined outside production and repro-duction. The institutions of the law, social welfare, family organization, and so on, serve to keep us outside productive/reproductive life. Our identity as *gay* is experienced by ourselves and others as in a very different relationship to our identity as worker or parent (or relative). The space we occupy and the space in which we must struggle is therefore primarily the space outside of 'necessity', the space of culture.

IDENTITY

If 'the homosexual' is a social category, then it is evident that actual people who fall into that category are going to be identified with and by it. People grow up to learn that they are homosexual or queer, or gay, and it is with this homosexual identity that gay political culture must necessarily engage.

Gay politics is about transcending the historical category 'homosex-ual', but it has always been a mistake to imagine that there could be an immediate, magic transcendence, a sudden leap free from the cultural categories within which we think, feel, live and are. Gay politics has necessarily to start from the given category, even if it ultimately wishes to move beyond it. This is not just a question of the political distinction between tactics (accepting and defending the category) and strategy (transcending it). It is only by accepting the category that we can transcend it. This is not idly said. To deny the category is to avoid the actual reality of the situation, namely, that certain people are *placed* in the category 'homosexual', and to ignore a situation is the surest way of ensuring that it remains the same.

What is at stake, to begin with, is who controls the definition of the category. The key significance of the gay movement is that for the first time in living memory, gay people *themselves* determined that they would decide the definition. The major, though by no means wholly secure, victory of this process has been the social acceptance of the word 'gay'. To have reached a point where a word selected by an oppressed group to describe itself is used almost as normal not only on the left but very generally in the media and in conversation is an extraordinary achievement. It signals the first occasion that people designated as homosexual have turned round and determined that they would decide what it means to be so designated.

Struggles over words can often seem trivial. Endlessly correcting people's assumptions that I must be married or have a girlfriend is tiring for me and seems niggling to those I'm correcting. Yet such relentless-ness is needed to change ingrained habits of thought, for habits are so hard to change. Word struggles often have a wider resonance. I remem-ber going on a demonstration against the Industrial Relations Bill where people had placards saying 'We're here for the queer', an attack on the prime minister, Edward Heath. By asking (successfully) for them to be removed we made a connection between sexism and labour politics, all by objecting to a word. (Similarly, we should object to attacks on Thatcher for being female or on Reagan for being old – there's enough to attack without falling into sexism and ageism.)

Being socially categorized, and determining something of the form of that categorization, also provides the possibility of thinking in terms of collective action. It is by recognizing that one's problems are not unique, that one belongs to a social group, that one is able to think in terms of together changing a general situation rather than accepting a purely personal 'condition'. Gay cultural politics has been particularly important here in exploring new identities, new shared senses of who we are.

An example of what I mean are the debates in the gay movement that surround disco. Disco has been a major development in gay culture in the 1970s and the wider disco scene itself grew out of, and is still marked by, gay disco. It is probably the most widespread form of leisure activity that gays are involved in, as both a dance/music form of expression and a space for social and sexual contact. The precise form it takes is important for the gay movement, because that is where so many gays 'are at'. I mean this both literally and figuratively: gays are in discos in vast numbers, and disco culture means a lot to us. Disco is, quantitatively and qualitatively, where we can reach gay people. The discussions at gay movement meetings about disco are often apparently focused on problems of organization – for instance, whether to charge, whether to hold discos in a straight or a gay venue, who will supply the music, etc. But at bottom they are about the business of constructing a gay identity. Thus some people argue that we should take our cue from the existing gay scene saying that there are certain ways of coping, forms of friendship network, the gay bar or club serving as a kind of community, that we could learn from. And they also point out that the kind of music favoured, usually derived from black music, is in some sense a gay music, and hence already expressive of a gay identity. Others point to the exploitativeness and furtiveness of the gay scene, the predominance of men and masculine modes of behaviour, and want the gay movement to learn from the counter-culture and its life-styles. The result is alternative discos, at their best a creative fusion or interplay of both of these traditions. The experience of being with gay people is altered, for instance, if the discos are free, if people talk to each other, if they are obviously organized by other gay people, if women and men are equally welcome and made welcome, if people dance in circles instead of either isolated or in couples. Talking about and dancing to different sorts of music can explore or reinforce sexual identities. The wrangling about whether to let Donna Summer or the Rolling Stones predominate is a way of talking through what we want our identity to be. Summer represents disco, an already gay cultural form, at its most sensuous; the Stones represent rock 'n' roll at its most 'alternative' but also its most 'straight' (in sexual terms). They are emblematic of different ways of being. Discussing and dancing to them become the very activity of constructing a shared sense of who we are.

Another example which brings out the interplay between pre-political sub-cultural forms and the construction of new identities is the question of dress. Dress is always a significant aspect of a person, for it reveals class, gender, racial and other sub-cultural positions whether consciously or unconsciously. Importantly it indicates how the wearer inhabits those positions, how she/he feels about being in that social position. Dress is especially significant for gays since being gay doesn't actually of itself 'show' physically, and it is only through dress that we can make a statement about ourselves that, unlike a verbal pronouncement, is there all the time.

The gay movement could draw on styles of dress that were already developed in the gay sub-culture, for instance, various forms of drag and prettiness for men, of butch and dyke gear for women. These styles provided a ground for a gay cultural politics of dress. Even before it is self-consciously political, drag and dyke dress is a play with the signs of femininity and masculinity, with what is appropriate dress for 'real' women and men. Gay cultural politics, in its concern with dress, has kept putting these definitions of gender in question. I do not mean to imply that confrontationist drag and dyke gear necessarily makes onlookers think through their own gender identities. Cultural struggle does not work automatically like that, much as many fondly hope it does. But such tactics are part of a wider debate about how and what it is to be a man or a woman, and how the very definitions of femininity and masculinity are posited on heterosexuality. This is to make it sound like an intellectual issue. But the point is rather, that gay cultural politics actually involves considering how you dress, being sensitive to what you and others wear. And this means bearing a consciousness of the categories of gender and sexuality in the lived texture of appearances.

One could make a similar argument around the current 'masculinization' of the gay male style. Today, gay men are rather more likely to adopt a macho look than drag and prettiness. This too is in a sense a reversal of the signs of masculinity. Gender roles are crucially defined in terms of heterosexuality – 'men', as a social category, are people who screw 'women'. By taking the signs of masculinity and eroticizing them in a blatantly homosexual context, much mischief is done to the security with which 'men' are defined in society, and by which their power is secured. If that bearded, muscular beer-drinker turns out to be a pansy, however are you going to know the 'real' men any more? From this too stem the play, exaggeration and parody of much contemporary gay masculinization. The most widely known example of this is the disco group Village People, whose dress draws on all the stereotypes of ultra-masculinity in a camped-up flauntingly gay way (Figure 14.1). There is profound ambivalence in this development. I am not at all clear in my own mind how gay men do actually relate to this masculinization. It can be taken straight – as a worship of the signs of male power, as an attempt to prove 'I may be queer but I'm still a man'. But it *can* be taken ironically and reflexively too, and two things help to encourage this. One is the debate about dress that the gay movement set in motion. People go on talking about the significance of what they wear, and how it does or does not carry and reproduce male power in society. Secondly, there is camp, that characteristically gay repertoire of parody, wit, put-down and send-up. This remains a powerful strain in gay culture, and it has always shown both a great sensitivity to gender roles *as* roles and a refusal to take the trappings of femininity and masculinity too seriously. We have to try to understand the new macho look in relation to all the frames of reference, reactionary and subversive, that can inform it.

PLEASURE

Disco and dress are examples of the way that gay cultural politics is centrally concerned with the contestation of identities. These identities make collective action possible, as the much more confident burgeoning of gay culture with a strong activist current in the USA makes clear. Gay cultural politics is also about pleasure. There is a definite fit between the gay movement's basic concern with sexuality and the centrality of culture to its political practice. Both are to do with pleasure. However, pleasure remains a forbidden term of reference, particularly on the left. Pleasure is something you can *guiltily* have, or have after the important things, or get as a reward for doing other things. As itself a goal, it is still not, to speak paradoxically, taken seriously. And nowhere is this more true than on the left.

It was clear from the start that the gay movement was primarily and perhaps exclusively concerned with sexuality and the consequences of a particular choice of sexuality. The women's movement has also been centrally concerned with sexuality, but women *as* women are not oppressed uniquely or even primarily in terms of their sexual desires but in terms of not being men. Struggles around housework, equal pay, job opportunities and so on do not spring directly from sexual activity. Even those struggles that are essentially concerned with sexuality somehow manage to couch themselves in other terms. Thus, issues of contraception, abortion and nursery facilities tend to run together and to be argued for in terms of what constitutes sane and healthy childcare and how such things free women in relation to paid employment, creativity and so on, rather than in terms of such things making sexuality less attendant with procreative anxiety, more controllable, more *enjoyable*. I

Figure 14.1 The Village People

know that that argument is there, but none the less that is not, over-all, how the debates around the issues developed. None of this could be said of gay movement issues. Queer-bashing, police harassment, discrimination in employment, treatment in the media, and all the other areas of gay activism may have the same civil rights flavour, but they all stem from the assertion of the right to a certain form of sexual activity. Nor was the gay movement merely demanding the right and need to love members of the same sex, but to enjoy sex with them. When in 1972 the Birmingham Gay Liberation Front produced the first British gay sex education pamphlet, *Growing Up Homosexual*, pleasure was listed as the first and overriding function of sex, above the ex-pression of love and (a poor third) procreation. Many in the move-ment pushed further, to insist that promiscuity, one-night stands, masturbation, forms of sexuality with minimal, attenuated, or non-existent human relationship elements, were as valid as, or more valid than, monogamy, affairs and love. They were seen as being in some sense more 'direct' and 'honest', less involved in manipulation and hypocrisy.

As Simon Watney points out, the Gay Liberation Front (GLF), which was the most vocal and 'radical' of the gay movement's various forms, saw sexuality as very much more than a particular activity. Sexuality was seen as the key that would unlock the fragmentation and alienation of advanced capitalist patriarchy.

Gay Liberation attempted to recuperate an illusion. That illusion maintained that our sexuality is the single most determining aspect of our entire existence.

(1980: 72)

He argues persuasively that a great deal more was felt to be at stake in struggling around sexuality than the pleasure of sexual activity for itself. This is clear too from Aubrey Walter's introduction to *Come Together*, a selection of articles from the GLF newspaper (1980) – though he is less critical of GLF's position than is Simon Watney. But GLF was not the whole gay movement, and a far more widespread impulse behind the various gay political activities of the 1970s was the assertion of the pleasure of sexuality and the right to that pleasure.

The problem was, again, definition: how to define sexuality. In practice, it meant genital, orgasmic sexuality. In the relation between women and men in the gay movement, this led to some pretty conundrums. On the one hand, in the sexual ideology we inherited, genital sexuality was 'masculine': women were supposed to be: romantic, their genital sexuality ineluctably intertwined with love; mysterious, their sexuality not physiologically locatable; or vaginal, a non-starter orgasmically (though not necessarily experienced as such (cf. McIntosh 1976)). Male gay culture teetered for a long time on the brink of this inheritance. Some of us wanted to insist on wider notions of sexuality, perhaps feeling there was something to learn from these definitions of female sexuality. Thus there were references to the 'tyranny of the orgasm' and a rejection of the instrumental, goal-oriented approach to coupling. Others wanted to expand the area of genital sexuality, to insist on the validity of more and 'purely' sexual genital activity. Many women were bored by this internal male debate and also put off by the obsession with genitals.

On the other hand . . . I remember talking to a woman friend of mine about the tyranny of the orgasm and being told, 'Don't knock orgasms – it took some of us a long time to get them.' To move beyond genital sexuality is an achievement for some men; to achieve genital sexuality can be a move beyond for some women.

We have certainly not succeeded in unpicking these contradictions, and this is partly because the whole debate, the very use of the word 'sexual', is still not extricated from the very ideology, discussed above, that separates genital sexuality from the rest of the body. Once this separation happens we are left in a quandary, having to choose between either genitality ('masculine') or emotionality ('feminine'), with no room for anything in between. Like the wider culture of heterosexual permissiveness, much of male gay culture, with its panoply of commercially supported saunas, bars, clubs and cruising places, is always in danger of simply wanting to expand genitality, simply to want more and more of it or to give it the creative power to transcend the present order. A danger, however, is not the whole story. Much that is happening is also seeking to break down the category 'sexuality', understood as *'genital* sexuality', and replace it with a new understanding and experience of the body in human existence.

BODY POLITICS

Many aspects of gay culture are a body culture, discovering and constructing new possibilities for the body. Disco and dress, already discussed, are in part about, respectively, the pleasure to be gained from using all one's body and the meanings to be constructed in the imaginative use of dress as body decoration. Massage and body awareness groups actively and consciously produce knowledge of what the body is and can be. More open kissing and hugging between men and men, women and women, are part of the style of the gay movement, both as a public sign that we are gay, but also as a pleasurable experience of friendship and solidarity. Such things begin to create a culture that refuses to refuse the body any more.

Many may well want to label all this bourgeois individualism. Doesn't it smack of California, where the sun always shines and people vote for Reagan? Isn't it the most gross self-indulgence in an age of mass unemployment and economic recession? Certainly it is hard to keep one's eyes on the wider goals of sexual politics when these immediate, hard issues face one. And yet to refuse this explanation of the body is simply to buy back into the cycle of body control that *constitutes* contemporary society.

Society isn't one thing and the human body another. Society is the organization of the human body, how we experience our bodies and what we do to and with them. The human body is a basic unit in any social formation. The paid worker's body, the houseworker's body remain the essential elements of any economy, of any maintenance and reproduction of life. In this society, the use of our bodies is compartmentalized: certain limbs and organs are used for work and nothing else, while pleasure is focused on an ever-narrowing range of 'erogenous' areas. Except when they occur in important activities such as sport and dance, all other body potentials are unknown, unrecognized, marginalized. Such compartmentalization produces body units that are easy to control; it rationalizes the fluidity and range of body potential. It also makes of the body something easier to place in economic exchange relations. It is easier to buy a person's body skill than her/his whole body. It is easier to sell pleasure if you are trying to appeal to one clearly defined region of the body.

This last point has led to the greatest confusion in the development of male gay sexual practices in the past ten years. Because the early gay movement put so much emphasis on genital sexuality, it was easy for capitalism to meet its demands. Bars, saunas, pornography, all the institutions of permissiveness, could seem like an answer to the demand for the liberation of sexuality. As long as sexuality meant genital sexuality, it could be quantified and its 'needs' met – more opportunities to do it more often. (There is a similar ideology in women's magazines like *Cosmopolitan*, though not in lesbian publications.) Our mistake, which we are only just beginning to see, was in demanding the liberation of sexuality, when we need to be demanding liberation *from* sexuality, in the name of the body.

The women's movement has long recognized the political importance of the body. Struggles around contraception, abortion, wife-battering and rape are not just 'issues' to form the basis of verbal, moral discussion nor are they only – though this they crucially are – assertions of the individual's right to determine what happens to her body. They also make us see how the very organization of procreation, the family and sexuality in society is done with, through and often to women's *bodies*. Though men find this especially hard to come to terms with and live with, such organization is also done with, through and to their own bodies. Men's physical frustrations and anxieties may have ideological or psychic roots, but where they get expressed is the body.

Ignorance of this on the left constitutes a denial of the body that is fatal for the movement. It means that we neither know our bodies for what they are and can be, nor do we operate effectively in and with them. In an immediate sense, denial of the body may simply make us less efficient in day-to-day political work: more liable to be tired, to be late, to be irritable, to be uncomradely. In the long term, denial of the body means that we do not take possession of our bodies politically.

'Body politics' is not an idle phrase. It points to the way in which society attempts to make over every person into a cog in an efficient system that at the same time fragments any control or knowledge we may have over or of our bodies. Our bodies are the site of control and power. We are not disembodied economic counters or ideological constructs. Lack of body politics has allowed left theory to lurch through various kinds of idealism, though each one calls itself materialist.

On the one hand, Marxism can degenerate into economic determinism. This may *appear* very materialist, because it is dealing with the 'hard' realities of money and work, but it deals with these realities in an abstracted, idealist way. Economic determinism reduces everything to the economic rather than seeing things *in relation to* the economic (and much else besides). It does designate economic categories and chart economic structures, but frequently fails to connect with the realities of factory and office life, the problems of getting and spending money. In other words, it fails to understand how economic structures are *lived and affected* in the skin and bones of people working.

On the other hand, recent Marxist theorists have rightly rejected such economic reductionism. But in their search for an alternative theory, they have come up with one that is equally prone to idealism. Working from theories of language and from psychoanalysis of a certain kind, they have put a valuable stress on the role of ideology in history, and, in particular, on the way people are socially formed into what we understand people to be – what is called 'the construction of the subject'. Yet their theory leads to a position where being 'a person' or 'a subject' is *only* a construction in language and ideology. Granted that society fashions us through words and representations of humanness, but it fashions us out of flesh and blood, not thin air.

None of this means that what the human body is is simply what 'nature' makes it. To go back to the point made at the beginning of this article, the biological activity of pleasurable bodily contact between persons of the same sex does not automatically give us the concepts 'sexuality' and 'the homosexual'. Those concepts are attempts to make sense (however, in this case, cock-eyed . . .) out of what are real biological activities. What is at stake is that, first, we are animals and can learn something about our bodies from biology. Second, that whatever else may come into play in the organization of our animal bodies to become specifically human bodies, we none the less remain in those bodies and had better learn about them: learn about what is biologically given, what is ideologically fashioned in them, if we want to be effective in history. And being effective in history is a cornerstone of what I take socialism to be about.

Gay culture, even when fully informed by sexual and socialist politics, does not have all the answers. But it does ask some of the questions, it does begin to think through not only gay identities, but *all* sexual and gender identities, and not only to think them through but to live them through the culture of the body. By so doing we make the very stuff of the social formation, our bodies, less amenable to prevailing power structures, more resistant to oppressive definitions and maimed existences. And in the pleasure we get we also get a glimpse of the other end of the rainbow.

NOTE

This chapter was originally published in George Bridges and Rosalind Brunt (eds) *Silver Linings*, London: Lawrence & Wishart, 1981.

REFERENCES

McIntosh, Mary (1976) 'Sexuality', *Papers on Patriarchy*, Lewes, Sx: Women's Publishing Collective, 73–5.
Marx, Karl (1977) 'The eighteenth brumaire of Louis Bonaparte', in Karl

Marx and Friedrich Engels, *Selected Works*, London: Lawrence & Wishart, 93–179.

Walter, Aubrey (1980) *Come Together*, London: Gay Men's Press.

Watney, Simon (1980) 'The ideology of GLF', in Gay Left Collective (eds) *Homosexuality: Power and Politics*, London: Allison & Busby, 64–76.

FURTHER READING

Bersani, Leo (1989) 'Is the rectum a grave?', in Douglas Crimp (ed.) *AIDS: Cultural Analysis, Cultural Activism*, Cambridge, MA: MIT Press, 197–222.

Bristow, Joseph (1989) 'Being gay: politics, identity, pleasure', *New Formations* 9: 61–81.

Bronski, Michael (1984) *Culture Clash: the Making of a Gay Sensibility*, Boston, MA: South End Press.

Cohen, Derek and Dyer, Richard (1980) 'The politics of gay culture', in Gay Left Collective (eds) *Homosexuality: Power and Politics*, London: Allison & Busby, 172–86.

Jay, Karla and Young, Allen (eds) (1978) *Lavender Culture*, New York: Harcourt, Brace, Jovanovich.

Shepherd, Simon and Wallis, Mick (eds) (1989) *Coming On Strong: Gay Politics and Culture*, London: Unwin Hyman.

Weeks, Jeffrey (1985) *Sexuality and its Discontents*, London: Routledge & Kegan Paul.

Weeks, Jeffrey (1986) *Sexuality*, London: Tavistock.

Index

abundance 20, 24, 25, 26
Adventures of Marco Polo, The 80
Afro-American culture 153; *see also*
    black culture
Aitken, Will 124
All That Heaven Allows 95, 96
Altman, Dennis 146
American Theater Ballet 20, 28
Andrews, Julie 46, 51, 52, 54–7
Another Time, Another Place 92
art 12, 31, 44, 110, 143; and education
    13, 14; and entertainment 3, 12, 28;
    and revolution 157; socialist 114
artistic sign 46
Astaire, Fred 20, 27, 28, 32
authenticity 23, 94–5, 97

Bachelor in Paradise 91
Bad and the Beautiful, The 65, 66,
    79–80, 87–91, 94, 97
Balanchine, George 41, 42
Banks-Smith, Nancy 143
Basinger, Jeanine 66, 69, 91
Bassey, Shirley 21
BBC 13–14, 15
Beardsley, Aubrey 137, 138
Beatles, the 14
Benson, George 154
Berkeley, Busby 20, 70, 137, 144
Big Cube, The 91
'Big Spender' 62, 64
Birmingham Gay Liberation Front 168
Birmingham Gay Men's Socialist
    Group 131
black: communities 32; culture 22, 32,
    96–7, 145; dance groups 43; dancers
    in classical ballet 42; music 153–4,
    164; people 6, 18, 25; power 110,
    112
black men 110–14; in gay

pornography 122
Bloch, Ernest 33
body, the 122–3, 159–60, 161; in
    Christian iconography 132; in
    classical ballet 41, 43, 44; in gay
    culture 169–72; politics 171
Body Politics 103
Bogart, Humphrey 117
Bow, Clara 69
Brecht, Bertolt 33
burlesque 74

Cabaret 58
Cabin in the Sky 32
Calling Dr Kildare 67
Call Me Madam 56
camp 135–47; humour 25; sensibility
    138, 144–5; straight 145
Campaign for Homosexual Equality
    (CHE) 136
capitalism 18, 25, 151; and music
    149–52; and pornography 121, 132;
    and sexuality 170
'carnivalesque' 6
Carousel 58
Cass Timberlaine 88
character: construction 65, 75; in
    quality drama 36
Chinatown 76
Church, the 12, 151
cinematic treatment 30, 65
Clark, Petula 149
class 25; and classical ballet 43; and
    images of male power 110–14; and
    Julie Andrews 55; and ordinariness
    98; and pornography 124; and *The
    Sound of Music* 56, 58
classical ballet 20, 41–3, 137; and
    choreography 43; and collectivity
    41; and Covent Garden 41, 42; and

evening classes 41, 42; and
  femininity 43; in gay culture 43;
  and racism 43; and state
  communisms 42; in the USA 43;
  and whiteness 42, 43
Clift, Montgomery 107
'Climb Every Mountain' 47, 57, 58, 59
Clooney, Rosemary 149
Cole, Nat King 94
Colt models 145
comedy 14, 122
Come Together 168
common sense 1
communication: non-verbal 103
community 21, 24, 156, 164
'Confidence' 46, 52, 59
consumerism 25, 157; as spectacle 24
contradiction: and disco 156; and
  entertainment 25
Cosmopolitan 170
Crawford, Joan 58
Crisp, Quentin 135
Critique of 'The School Wives', The 7, 11
Crosby, Bing 21
cultural politics 159, 162; *see also* gay
  cultural politics culture 2, 161–3;
  high culture 4, 20; see also popular
  culture

dance 20, 132; in *The Sound of Music*
  56
Davis Jr, Sammy 61
Defiant Ones, The 130
de Havilland, Olivia 59
desire 4
Detroit Spinners 154
Dietrich, Marlene 138, 149
Dietz, Howard and Schwartz, Arthur
  11, 12
disco 149–58; and capital 150–2;
  dancing 154; and eroticism 142–4,
  157; and fashion 156; and feminism
  and socialism 157; in gay culture
  164, 165, 166, 169; and
  materialism 157–8; romanticism 154–7
discourse 2; analysis 123, 132
'Dixit Dominus' 46, 49
'Do Re Mi' 47, 53, 54
Douglas, Kirk 87
Dramatic School 67
dress 25, 161; in gay cultural politics
  165–6, 169; and Village People
  166–7; *see also* fashion; *haute
  couture*

Duncan, Isadora 132
Dunne, Irene 59
Dworkin, Andrea 122

Eco, Umberto 19
editing: in *The Sound of Music* 48–9,
  52–3; in *Sweet Charity* 61
energy 20, 23, 25, 31, 32–3
entertainment i, ix-x, 1–4, 5–6, 7–8,
  11–15, 17; and bourgeois
  amusement 13; in broadcasting 14;
  and contradiction 25; and cultural
  production 1, 8, 151–2; escape 7,
  18, 30; and ideology 5–6; and
  medieval Europe 12; and politics ix,
  x, 2; and society 2, 18; and the
  urban working class 13; and utopia
  7, 17–33
Enzensberger, Hans Magnus 23–5
Epstein, Edward Z. *see* Morella, Joe
ethnicity 110; and pornography 124

fashion 20, 32, 142, 149; in disco 159;
  see also dress; *haute couture*
Faust, Beatrice 125, 127
female sexuality 128
femininity 92, 165, 168
Fields, Gracie 21
film: aesthetic 121; analysis 22; state-
  funded 3; studies ix, 3, 4
Film Night (BBC 2) 143
films noirs 75–6
Firbank, Ronald 138
folk culture 20; in *The Sound of Music*
  56, 57
folk music 149, 150, 157
Fonteyn, Margot 41, 42
Fortunes of War 36, 37
Fosse, Bob 61
Freud, Sigmund 108; Freudian ideas
  101
Funny Face 20, 27, 28–9, 30–1
Funny Girl 52, 58

Gable, Clark 75, 88
Gardner, Ava 86, 91
Garland, Judy 21, 25, 66, 69, 71, 74,
  94
Garson, Greer 58
gay: cultural politics 162, 163, 164,
  165, 166; culture 159, 161, 164, 166,
  169, 172, and the arts 161, and
  classical ballet 42, and the gay
  movement 161-2; identity 152; male

culture 152, 155, 168–9; male
    politics 121; male sexual practice
    121, 170; and music 149, 154; *see
    also* gay movement; gay
    pornography
Gay Liberation Front (GLF) 136, 167–8
gay movement, the 128, 163, 165, 167,
    168, 169, 170
Gay News 142
Gaynor, Gloria 153, 154
gay pornography (male) 121–34; and
    film 125–31; and police practices
    132; *see also* pornography
Gay Rights at Work Committee 162
gender: and classical ballet 43; and
    muscularity 114
Generation Game, The 1
genre 61, 121–2
Gershwin, George 152
Gigi 32
Giles, Dennis 128
glamour 79, 87
Golddiggers of 1933, 20, 26, 27, 30–1
Gombrich, E. H. 19
Gone With the Wind 59
Growing Up Homosexual 167
Gypsy 58

Hallelujah! 32
Hamlet 12
Hancock, Herbie 154
haute couture 20, 71, 91–2; *see also*
    dress; fashion
Hayes, Isaac 154
Heath, Edward 164
hedonism, born-again ix, 7
Hello Dolly! 32
Hepburn, Audrey 28, 31, 32
Homecoming 88
'homosexual' 159–61, 171
Honky Tonk 75
Hudson, Rock 95, 96
Hunter, Ross 91

iconography 121, 132
idealism 123, 132, 171
identity 136; as gay 152, 163, 164, 171;
    homosexual 161, 163–6
ideology ix, 3, 5, 65, 162, 171; and
    capitalist production 121, 151; and
    disco 149; dominant 25; and Lana
    Turner 97–8; and music 151; and

porn stars 132; and *The Sound of
    Music* 45, 46, 48, 58
'If My Friends Could See Me Now'
    61, 64
'I Love to Cry at Weddings' 64
'I'm a Brass Band' 61, 64
Imitation of Life 65, 66, 91–7; and
    acting 94
Industrial Relations Bill
    demonstration 163–4
intensity 20, 22, 24, 25
I Remember Mama 59
ITV 13, 14
'I've Got You Under My Skin' 153,
    154

Jackson, Mahalia 96–7
James, Clive 143
Jameson, Fredric 33
Je tu il elle 127
Jewel in the Crown, The 38
Jones, Grace 153, 154–5
Jones, Quincy 154
jouissance 6
Jump Cut 131

Kaye, Danny 31
Keeler, Howard 21
Keep Your Powder Dry 74
Kelly, Paula 64
King and I, The 57, 58
King's Rhapsody 56
Kojak 145
Kuhn, Annette 8

Labelle, Patti 154
labour 2, 114; politics 164
Labour Party 151
Lady from Shanghai, The 76
Lamarr, Hedy 66, 69, 71, 74
Lanallure 79, 93
Lana: the Life and Loves of Miss Turner
    66
Langer, Susanne K. 19, 22, 46
Latin Lovers 91, 92
L.A. Tool and Die 129–30
Lee, Peggy 149
Leigh, Vivian 59
leisure 2, 13, 32, 114, 156, 162; park
    20
Leonard, Robert Z. 69
lesbian mothers, campaign around
    162
lesbian sexuality 128

Life of Her Own, A 91, 92
Linton, James 5, 6
'Lonely Goatherd, The' 47, 53, 54, 56
looking 103–4, 108
Love Finds Andy Hardy 67
Love Has Many Faces 65, 91, 92
Lovell, Terry 6, 121, 132, 151

MacDonald, Jeanette 137, 138, 141
MacLaine, Shirley 62, 63, 64
Madame X 65, 91
male: heterosexuality 108; sexuality
    121, 127; *see also* gay male sexual
    practice
Maltese Falcon, The 76
Man Made Language 103
Marcuse, Herbert 25, 156
'Maria' 46, 47, 48, 49
Marriage is a Private Affair 74–5
Marx, Karl 159; Marxism 2, 170, 171
Mary Poppins 54, 55
masculinity 110, 114–19, 137, 164,
    165, 168; and porno-graphy 124
mass media and manipulation 24
Masters and Johnson 125
materialism 31; and disco 157–8; in
    politics 157
Mathis, Johnny 149
Mead, Margaret 127
Meat 124
media, the 1, 145, 168
media studies 4
Meet Me in St Louis 32
melodrama 95, 122
men 31, 165
Merman, Ethel 25
Merry Widow, The 32, 56, 91
Mildred Pierce 58
Miller, Ann 29, 30, 33
Minnelli, Vincente 87, 89
'Mirror Fella' 105
mise-en-scène 65, 75; criticism 22
Molière 7, 11, 12
Monroe, Marilyn 98
Moore, Juanita 95
More, Thomas 18
Morella, Joe and Epstein, Edward Z.
    66, 69, 88, 89
Morris, William 18
Moses (Michelangelo) 104
Movie 22
Mrs Miniver 58
Murdoch, Rupert 35, 39
Muscle Beach 125, 126

muscularity 114–5
music 19; and capitalism 149; and
    ideology 151; in *Mary Poppins* 55; in
    The Sound of Music 48, 49, 52–4, 56,
    59
musicals 17, 25, 30, 56, 58, 61, 70,
    121; backstage 11, 30; and escape
    30; and narrative 33; Rodgers and
Hammerstein 57, 58
Muybridge, Eadweard 110
My Fair Lady 32, 54, 55
'My Favourite Things' 46–7, 52, 54,
    59; and editing 52–3
My Guy 104
My Secret Life 127

Naked Civil Servant, The 135
narrative 33, 65, 70; and pornography
    125–31; and *The Sound of Music* 46,
    57; and *Sweet Charity* 61
Naughty Marietta 56
Navy Blue 130
Newman, Paul 108, 109
news, the 17, 20, 22
New York City Ballet 41
non-representational, the 25, 26, 28,
    33; and *The Sound of Music* 45–6
non-verbal communication 103
novel, the eighteenth century, 21
Nude Male, The 116
Nureyev, Rudolf 41

Oedipus Rex 12
Oh Boy! 104, 108, 114
Oliver! 32
'one-dimensional' 25; *One-Dimensional
    Man* 156
On the Town 20, 24, 29, 30, 32–3
ordinariness 79, 98

Peirce, C. S. 19
performance 20, 75, 87; sign 19, 22
Peyton Place 65, 92, 94
phallus, the 116, 119
Phillips, Esther 154
pin-up, the male 103–19; Lana Turner
    as 79–80, 81, 82, 83, 84, 85; pin-ups
    ix-x, 99
plaisir 6
Playboy 104
Playgirl 104, 111, 118
Playguy 145
pleasure ix-x, 2, 4, 5–7, 162;
    gay/homosexual 161, 166–9, 172;

and pornography 124; and quality drama 35, 36; radical 6; *see also jouissance; plaisir*
Plummer, Christopher 46, 50
Poitier, Sidney 114
political struggle 150, 156
popular culture 2, 4, 6, 8
popular song 152–3, 154, 155
populism 12, 15
Porgy and Bess 32
pornography 6, 121, 122, 132, 170; in counter-cinema 129; and erotica 122, 132; feminist criticism of 122; as a genre 123; and left culture 121, 131
Porter, Cole 152, 153, 154
Portrait in Black 91
Postman Always Rings Twice, The 65, 74–8, 79, 89, 97
poverty 23, 30, 31
Presley, Elvis 149
Prince of Wales, the 114
Prodigal, The 91, 92
psychoanalysis 4–5; Lacanian 4, 5, 8, 123; and religion 5
Pym, Barbara 35

quality drama 35–9; and world-historical events 36–4
Queen Mother, the 138, 139
queens 136, 137
'queer' 163, 164

Rains of Ranchipur, The 92
Reagan, Ronald 164
realist aesthetic 26
representation, modes of 19
representational, the 26, 28, 29, 33, 45; and *The Sound of Music* 45
Reynolds, Burt 145
rhythm 153, 154; *see also* signs, non-representational
Rivera, Chita 64
rock music 17, 150–1, 153, 157
rock'n'roll 8, 149, 150, 153, 165
Roger 125–6
Rogers, Ginger 29
Rolling Stones 149, 164, 165
Ross, Diana 155
Rutsky, R. L. and Wyatt, Justin 6

St Denis, Ruth 132
Saturday Night Fever 155, 156
Sayers, Janet 132

Schlupmann, Heide 2
Schwarz, Arthur *see* Dietz, Howard
Schwarzenegger, Arnold 113, 114
Scrooge 32
Sea Chase, The 92
Seagers, Will 129, 130
sexuality 108, 114, 121, 124, 127, 129, 132, 160–1, 168–9, 170–1; and Julie Andrews 55; lesbian 128; and pornography 122; and the women's movement 166; *see also* male sexuality
She 104, 111; 'She-Male' 104
Shean, Al 71
show business 11, 18, 25; show-biz 17, 20, 28
signs, non-representational 18–19; representational 18–19, 22; *see also* performance
Sinatra, Frank 91
Sirk, Douglas 95
Sleeping Beauty, The 138
soap opera 8, 17, 123; and quality drama 35, 36
social tension 23
Somewhere I'll Find You 75
Son of the Sheik, The 99–102
Song of Norway 32, 56
Sontag, Susan 138
soul 146, 149
Sound of Music, The 23, 45–59
'Sound of Music, The' 46, 47, 48, 49, 53, 54; and editing 48–9
South Pacific 57, 58
sport 114
star image 65, 75; and Lana Turner 80, 97; in pornography 132
Star is Born, A 58
stars 18, 21, 65, 97; and contradiction 66
Straight to Hell 124
style professions 138, 140
subject, the 171
Summer, Donna 155, 164–5
Sun, The 104
Sweet Charity 58, 61–4

Tamla Motown 149
Tanner, Elsie 25
tap dance 20, 22
Tarnished Angels, The 95
television: as escape 13–14; light entertainment 14, 15; spectaculars 17; Thatcherite 35

Temptations, The 154
Thank God It's Friday 157
Thatcher, Margaret 164
'That's Entertainment' 11, 12
They Won't Forget 66–7, 76
Thirkell, Mark 129
Three Musketeers, The 88
Tom of Finland 143, 145
'Touch Me in the Morning' 155
Tracy, Spencer 88
transparency 21, 22, 23, 25
Turner, Lana 65–98; and marriage 67, 74, 88, 91; and Stompanato, Johnny 91, 94

utopia 29, 33; utopianism 18, 33, 130; utopian sensibility 20–1, 22–3, 25

Valentino, Rudolph 99, 100, 102n, 106
Variety 11, 17, 25, 33, 42
vaudeville 22, 31, 64, 71
Village People 154, 166, 167
virility 95
Viva 115

Wagner, Richard 138
Wanted 130

Wayne, John 92, 138, 143, 144
weepies 3, 121, 122
Westerns 3, 17, 20, 22, 121
We Who Are Young 67
white: culture 96; men 110–14
White Christmas 31
White Hero, Black Beast 104
Who's Got the Action? 91
Williams, Billy Dee 112
Williams, Raymond 46
Willis, Ellen 132
Wise, Robert 53
woman's film, the 4, 58, 91; and *The Sound of Music* 58
women 18, 25, 33, 165; women's movement, the 166, 170; women's struggles 166, 170
Wonder, Stevie 154
work 2, 13, 23, 114, 156
Written on the Wind 95
Wyatt, Justin *see* Rutsky, R. L.

'You Stepped out of a Dream' 71, 72

'Zerstreuung' 2, 6
Ziegfeld 20
Ziegfeld Girl 65, 66–7, 69–74, 79, 89, 97